BERLITZ®

FLORIDA

D0995968

- A ☑ in the text denotes a highly recommended sight
- A complete A–Z of practical information starts on p. 116
- Extensive mapping throughout: on cover flaps and in text

Printed in Switzerland by Weber SA, Bienne.

1st Edition (1993/1994)

Although we make every effort to ensure the accuracy of the information in this guide, changes do occur. If you have any new information, suggestions or corrections to contribute, we would like to hear from you. Please write to Berlitz Publishing at the above address.

Text: Martin Gostelow

Editor: Tanya Colbourne

Photography: Jacques Bétant, Aram Gesar, Martin Gostelow

Cartography: **Falk** Falk-Verlag, Hamburg

Layout: Visual Image

We wish to thank the following for their assistance with the preparation of this book: British Airways, Lee County Visitor and Convention Bureau, Greater Miami Convention and Visitors Bureau, Naples Area Chamber of Commerce, Spaceport USA, Universal Studios Florida and Walt Disney World Co.

CONTENTS

Florida and the Floridians

The south-east corner of the United States juts so far south it almost reaches the tropics. Almost 400 miles (640 km) long and roughly 130 miles (200 km) wide, this sun-drenched peninsula is so fringed by offshore islands hat its total coastline is practically trebled. The climate has enticed everyone – from multi-millionaires to pensioners on a tight budget; sports stars to student 'spring-breakers'; and refugees fleeing the arctic winters of Canada and the northern United States.

Florida matches California as a pacesetter in new ideas about fashion and entertainment, and Floridians enjoy a lifestyle only made possible by the generous gifts of nature. Film makers, businesses and high-technology enterprises have all been persuaded to move here. Even Mickey Mouse has taken up residence! And the Sunshine State has gone international, drawing the most unlikely combination of immigrants and tourists – a mosaic of sun-starved European holiday-makers, South American moguls and immigrants from the islands of the Caribbean.

Florida reinvents itself with every generation, from steaming swamp to tourist magnet to den of corruption, from retirement home to space base and back again to holiday paradise. Each time, something of the previous incarnation remains. The result is a kind of schizophrenia – it doesn't know whether to be sleepy and subtropical or fast and trendy. You'll be constantly jolted by the contrasts. Great wealth is juxtaposed with dire poverty; concrete sprawl adjoins impenetrable jungle; fine art stands hand-in-hand with kitsch; beaches throng with the obese and the svelte. Even the traffic seems to reflect this dichotomy – dreamers in cruise control versus the daredevil exhibitionists on the Miami freeways.

The most southerly of the continental states (only Hawaii is closer to the equator), Florida **5** endures scorching summers when you'll be greeted by a blast of heat and humidity. The reward comes in the form of mild winters when locals and visitors smugly read about fog and snow dislocating the cities of the north, while Miami basks in the nation's highest temperatures and the citrus crop ripens on the trees.

Florida's magnificent beaches — idyllic playground for children and adults alike.

Topographically Florida is more subtle in its appeal, a flat plain with the highest point a mere 345 ft (105 m) above sea level. The coastline is longer than any state's save Alaska and is wonderfully varied. A chain of offshore islands shields the Intra-Coastal Waterway. All along the coast, pelicans patrol above the waves, occasionally plummeting in a crash-dive when they spot a fish. Giant turtles can be seen wading ashore, while exquisite shells roll in the surf.

Along the Gulf Coast sweep miles of palm-fringed white sandy beaches, whose shallow waters provide safe bathing for children. The Atlantic beaches are more golden, with the chance of bigger waves appealing to surfers. The water is warm thanks to the Gulf Stream, making it a paradise for anyone who loves water recreation.

Inland, grassy plains shimmer with an estimated 30,000 lakes. The landscape is divided by cattle ranches, fragrant orange groves, pine and cypress forests and homely small towns.

Exotic flowers are not restricted to the many lush botanical gardens. In this climate anyone can grow them. From the lakes, the overflow of warm water seeps south and west through hundreds of square miles of grassland culminating in the mangrove swamps of the Everglades – pride of southern Florida. Here you can sail, canoe, fish or explore the trails in search of alligators, southern bald eagles or (probably in vain!) the elusive Florida panther.

A holiday in Florida provides every opportunity to try your hand at a host of outdoor sports. Water-skiing, scuba-diving, surfing, tennis, golf or riding – whatever appeals to you, you may be sure friendly and professional instructors will be close at hand with advice. Many resorts feature video-equipped tennis and golf clinics with computer analysis of your faults. All types of spa facilities abound, offering exercise programmes, relaxing massages and bubbling jacuzzis.

Whatever your preference – be it exploring the mangrove **7**

The Ethnic Mix

Florida's kinship with the American Deep South can be felt most in the north of the state, around Tallahassee and Jacksonville – Anglo-Saxon in origin and with a large black population too. But from the time of its Spanish discovery, the state has always had a pronounced Latin flavour. Cuba is only 90 miles (145 km) from Key West, a fact which has often affected Florida's history and still does. Cuban exiles make up the largest contingent in Miami, lending great colour to the street life, spice to the cuisine and an edge to the politics. Even second-generation Cubans are fiercely loyal to a certain image of the 'old country', and vociferous about past and current events there. The Latin presence was further augmented by an influx of Nicaraguans during their homeland's troubles. And more recently still, there has been an increasing number of Caribbean immigrants, particularly from Haiti.

Florida is a magnet too for the New Yorker. Accents in the supermarkets and around the swimming pools of Miami Beach and the Gold Coast are more likely to be laced with the heavy ironies of Brooklyn and Queens than the good-ol'-boy cheerfulness of the neighbouring southern states of Georgia and Alabama. Italians, Greeks, Scandinavians running cruise lines, Brits hungry for sunshine – think of a national group and you'll find them here.

The Florida Keys have always attracted a cosmopolitan mixture of bohemians – artists, writers and seekers after the good life flock here from all over America and beyond. This lively bunch of eccentrics defy any ethnic classification at all.

Key West does have its own proud 'Conchs' (named after the shellfish). They trace their ancestry back to the American revolution when loyalists to the British crown fled first to the Bahamas and then on to the Keys, where their community still runs the fishing business and keeps aloof from 'interlopers'.

swamps, visiting the Kennedy Space Center or even admiring the world's largest collection of seashells – you'll be overwhelmed by the choice of things to see and do. Soon you'll become blasé about the 'World's Biggest' and 'World's Best' labels.

For most holiday-makers, eating is an important element in their enjoyment. Dining in Florida is informal and an indulgence undertaken with great gusto. Portions tend to be enormous and the famous 'all-you-can-eat' buffets provide a daunting challenge even to the most ardent gourmand. Eating and drinking goes on unabated at all times of the day and night. The variety is endless – choose stone crabs or a live lobster from a tank, go out to a traditional barbecue, or venture into one of Miami's Cuban restaurants in Little Havana for something really special.

Florida's appeal is immediate. More than that it grows on you. For the thousands who flock to the Sunshine State, exchanging overcoats and business suits for cut-off shorts and sports gear, there is the feeling that this is the place to be. Daiquiris in hand, the local Floridians will laugh and say they know the feeling well – it's called 'getting sand in your shoes'.

*P*eddle power in Coconut Grove.

A Brief History

The flat landscape of Florida emerged long ago from the sea, augmented by silt washed down by the mighty rivers of the north and coral reefs growing in the warm waters. In prehistoric times sabre-toothed tigers prowled through the wetlands. Woolly mammoths, giant bison and even camels roamed the plains.

The first humans arrived about 15,000 years ago, perhaps from further north, but possibly from Central America. They lived by hunting and fishing and especially from the generous supplies of shellfish. In south and central Florida, in fact, some of the highest hills are the oyster shell mounds piled up by these earliest inhabitants. Some of them can still be seen, although many disappeared in modern times

Facts and Figures

Population: 9,000,000.

Geography: 58,560 sq. miles (151,670 km) in area with the second-longest coastline of any US state (1,350 miles/2,170 km).

State Capital: Tallahassee (population 90,000).

Climate: Semi-tropical in the southern half of the state, less extreme in northern areas; sunshine can be relied upon most of the year; humidity may be very high in summer. Chance of hurricanes from June to November.

Economy: Tourism and service industries, citrus fruit and vegetable growing, cattle-raising, tobacco, food processing, chemicals, electrical and transportation equipment, space technology.

Get there: Jet flight from New York 2½ hours, London 9 hours.

when the material in them was used to make roads and tracks through the swamps.

By the standards of the times, these early Floridians had an easier life than most hunter-gatherers. Judging by surviving pieces, they had leisure to create artworks such as shell jewellery and beautiful statuettes. Ceremonial burials also suggest an organized religious life. Around 1450 BC, they found that despite the low-fertility soil, the climate made it possible to cultivate crops such as maize, squash, cassava, and peppers. Archaeologists have recently dated quite complex systems of drainage canals to that period.

On the eve of the European discovery of the New World, Florida's indigenous population numbered some tens of thousands, divided into five nations. Chief of these were the Timucua of the north, the Apalachee in the Panhandle and the Calusa in the south-west.

European Discovery

Columbus was not far from Florida when he bumped into the island of Hispaniola (now Haiti and the Dominican Republic) on his way to 'the Indies' in 1492. Other early explorers including the Cabot brothers may have searched the Florida coast for a passage to the Pacific, but credit for the discovery of the land goes to Juan Ponce de León (1460–1521). Bored with life in Spain after the Moorish wars ended, he set out with Columbus on his second expedition in 1493. The voyage rekindled his taste for adventure and by 1508 Ponce was on his way to Puerto Rico. He became the island's governor, but soon lost his position to the more influential Diego Columbus, son of the navigator.

In 1512, the Spanish king commissioned Ponce de León to find and explore the fabled 'Isle of Bimini'. The island, so legend said, concealed a spring with the miraculous power to restore youth to the aged. No doubt Ponce, 52 years old at the time, was inspired with hope. If it didn't work, there was still the prospect of gold and slave labour to provide for his old age.

Setting sail for the Bahamas in search of Bimini, Ponce landed instead on the Florida coast, on 2 April 1513. He named the new country after the date in his calendar, *Pascua Florida*, the Feast of Flowers at Easter. From his first landfall, near present-day St Augustine, Ponce and his crew sailed down the coast, past Cape Canaveral, along the Florida Keys and out to the Dry Tortugas. From there they continued north along the Gulf coast to Charlotte Harbor, and possibly beyond, before returning to Puerto Rico after an eight-month voyage. Ponce had missed Bimini, but he had found an immense land full of promise, which his grateful sovereign granted him the right to conquer, govern and colonize.

Blighted Hopes

Ponce's discovery was to prove a bitter disappointment to him. On a second voyage to Florida in 1521, the explorer took along two ships, 200 colonists, livestock and farm implements. Though Ponce knew from his first visit that the Calusa Indians at Charlotte Harbor were hostile, he chose to land there nevertheless. His party were in the process of building shelters when fierce warriors attacked. Ponce himself was badly wounded by an arrow, and was carried back to his ship. By the time the disillusioned settlers reached Cuba their leader was near death. He was buried in Puerto Rico.

The pattern of great expectations and dashed hopes was to repeat itself in later ventures. Pánfilo de Narváez, a follower of Cortés, set out from Cuba in 1528 with 600 soldiers and colonists, but quickly lost 200 of his party in skirmishes. Marching inland from Tampa Bay, they expected to find food and water easily, but in the event they almost starved. The fabled gold was nowhere to be found: the only inhabitants were poor Indian women and children living in mud huts. Panic-stricken in a strange and

*P*edro Menénez de Avilés, founder of St Augustine.

hostile land, Narváez and his followers built makeshift boats and set sail for Mexico, which they thought was nearby. The voyage was doomed from the outset. Of the 242 who manned the boats, only four ever reached Mexico City. Narváez was not among them. A search party sent out by Narváez's wife also disappeared.

Yet another ill-fated expedition was led by Hernando de Soto. Already rich and famous at the age of 36, the Spanish explorer left Cuba for Florida in 1538 with 600 optimistic volunteers. When they

PEDRO MENENDEZ DE AVILES
FOUNDER OF ST AUGUSTINE
1565

landed in Tampa Bay on 30 May 1539, they were met by Juan Ortiz, a survivor from the search party sent to find Narváez. Ortiz could now speak the Indian languages, and was to prove invaluable as a guide and interpreter. But this auspicious beginning was not followed by similar good fortune. Though de Soto's band marched as far as Oklahoma and Kansas in search of riches, they found none. The further they went, the more determined they became to continue until they discovered something, but they never did. Half of the men, including de Soto himself, died during the four-year odyssey. The survivors made their way back to Cuba empty-handed.

The First Permanent Settlement

Control of Florida's east coast became strategically important as soon as Spanish treasure fleets began to sail along it, following the Gulf Stream. News that France was taking an interest drove Spain at last to found a durable colony.

On 8 September 1565, Pedro Menéndez de Avilés and a detachment of soldiers arrived at the mouth of the St John's river near present-day Jacksonville, where a party of French Huguenots had been struggling along for a year in their small settlement at Fort Caroline.

At this time the two great European nations were engaged in a bitter contest for colonial domination, and a battle was certain. The French were caught by surprise, with their ships away at sea, and were easily overcome. Later, the French fleet was wrecked on the coast in a storm, and the Spaniards were able to round up the survivors. Faced with the problem of what to do with the captives, Menéndez decided that the threat to his own party with its limited food supply was too great to ignore. Sparing women and children, Catholics and musicians, he put the rest to the sword 'not as Frenchmen, but as Lutherans'.

About 30 miles (48 km) south of Fort Caroline, Menéndez founded the first permanent settlement in North America, the colony of St Augustine. It suffered from sporadic Indian attacks and in 1586 was raided by the English privateer Sir Francis Drake. The difficulties of defending the outpost were plain, but it was judged essential, and in response to later English, Indian and pirate assaults, the Spanish constructed a massive fortress of stone which still stands today.

Imperial Rivals

In 1682 Robert Cavelier Sieur de La Salle completed his long journey down the Mississippi, claiming the entire river valley for the King of France, Louis XIV. When Louis attempted to seat his grandson on the throne of Spain, England was quick to see the peril. Spain and France united could dictate to the rest of Europe and the world.

The War of the Spanish Succession in 1702 brought British forces deep into Florida. Though the fortress at St Augustine survived an eight-week siege and never fell, the British wiped out most of Spain's other military outposts and religious missions in four years of war.

With Spanish power in decline, Britain and France could concentrate on fighting each other for domination of North America. The Seven Years' War in Europe spread to the New World as the 'French and Indian War'. Despite Indian support, French forces went down in defeat, leaving the British as virtual masters of the continent. In 1763 Florida was officially ceded to Britain and the Spaniards moved out.

With the new European overlords came another shift in population. Descendants of the original American Indians, shattered by European diseases, the slave trade and internal feuds, left Florida with the Spaniards to find more peaceful homes in the West and Cuba. Their farms and villages were taken over by a mixture of tribes from Alabama and Georgia called the Seminoles (from the Spanish *cimarrones*, 'runaway' or 'wild').

The Seminoles were eagerly courted by British traders bearing pots, knives, guns and axes. The new government gave **15**

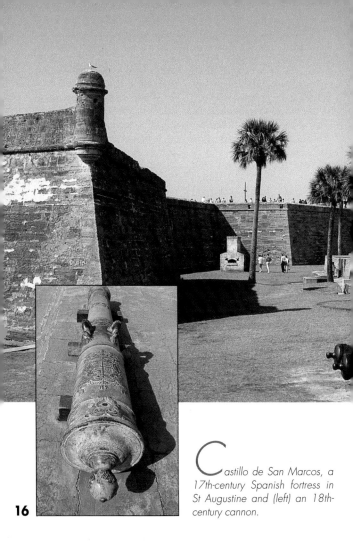

*C*astillo de San Marcos, a 17th-century Spanish fortress in St Augustine and (left) an 18th-century cannon.

Lost Colony

After the British defeat in the American War of Independence, Florida was returned to Spanish rule by the Treaty of Paris of 1783. But the allegiance of Florida's Seminole and European inhabitants remained with Britain, which had done so much to develop the land. In a further bizarre turn of events, the British, now allied with Spain in the Napoleonic wars, landed forces in western Florida in 1814, only to withdraw again when US troops, under the future president Andrew Jackson, marched into the disputed territory. Further American incursions marked this final unhappy spell of Spanish rule. Unable to control Florida, Spain ceded it to the United States in 1819. Jackson became its first US governor in 1821.

grants to enterprising colonists to organize plantations and soon indigo, rice, turpentine, sugar and oranges became lucrative exports. The British had found a way to make money where the Spanish had failed to find gold.

American settlers flooded into Florida, causing consternation among the long-time inhabitants. The Seminoles were gradually pushed off the fertile lands of the north and into the Everglades. Then in **17**

1830, Andrew Jackson, now president, signed an act of Congress ordering all American Indians to move to new lands in the frontier territories to the west. Some accepted; others stood and fought. In the Seminole War of 1835–42 it became clear that conventional US forces were unsuited to combating the hit-and-run tactics of opponents who could disappear into the steaming swamps of southern Florida. The Seminole leader Osceola was seized, although under a flag of truce at the time, and died in prison not long after. His followers did not give up the struggle but were forced deeper into the Everglades. The war ended at last in stalemate, but only a few hundred Seminoles remained, in small, scattered villages.

Civil War

With peace came growing prosperity, and in 1845, statehood, as the 27th member of the Union. There was a new wave of northern immigrants, but for the most part,.local power rested on plantation owners who depended on slave labour. Thus Florida took the side of the southern states in the American Civil War, seceding from the Union in 1861 and joining the Confederacy. But in a replay of the Spanish-British conflict, Union forces from the north easily captured and occupied most of Florida's ports and forts. Many Confederate troops were sent to fight distant battles and those that remained were mainly engaged in raiding supply lines.

With the war's end in 1865 came nominal freedom for the slaves, although many in fact continued to work for their former masters in scarcely better conditions. Their hopes for equal rights were dashed and Florida acquired a corrupt, segregationist state government. However, the war and its aftermath had brought the state to the attention of northern investors. It had suffered less destruction than the rest of the South and was to develop quite differently.

Whitehall, the Palm Beach mansion of railway baron Henry Flagler.

19

Railroad Barons and Early Tourists

By the last quarter of the 19th century, a number of enterprising businessmen had seen the potential of the state's geography and climate. Two names stand out: Henry Morrison Flagler and Henry Bradley Plant. Both possessed the kind of pioneering spirit that was the driving force of that expansionary era. What was more, they had the money to turn their dreams into reality. Flagler's East Coast Railroad drove through swamp and jungle, reaching Miami in 1896 and eventually spanning the ocean to Key West. Henry Plant's lines to Tampa and beyond opened up central and western Florida.

It didn't take long for the good news to spread, and before long tourists were descending in droves. Permanent settlers came too: between 1870 and 1890, Florida's population doubled, and it has continued to grow ever since. So has the pressure on land. It was the memorably named state governor, Napoleon Bonaparte Broward, who dug the first spadeful of earth in 1905 to begin a massive drainage programme. Hundreds of miles of canals and dikes converted huge tracts of the Everglades into dry land. Hailed at the time, it is now looked on as a disaster by conservationists, and limited attempts are being made to reverse the process in places.

The tourist boom became a near riot in the mid-1920s when real estate prices began to soar. Suddenly, thousands of Americans wanted to own a piece of Florida for vacations, retirement or just as an investment. Over 2,000 arrivals a day flooded into the state, and soon the railroads forbade any car to advertise Miami as its destination. Then, reality began to redress the balance. A ship from up north carrying would-be Floridians sank in Biscayne Bay; a hurricane in 1926 wrought havoc in the city; the bottom fell out of land prices, and with the onset of depression in 1929, the bonanza was over.

World War II and After

Florida's economy didn't really recover until the beginning of World War II when thousands of recruits arrived to be trained at the state's bases. These modern soldiers and sailors fell under the same spell as others before them. When peace came, remembering the warmth of the southern sun, many returned to Florida to start businesses, raise families, and later, to retire. The state's economy was diversified.

Hurricane Who?

Alice or Arthur? It used to be traditional to give women's names to hurricanes: now to avoid sexism, they alternate. But whatever people call them makes no difference to these frighteningly powerful tropical storms which sweep through Florida from time to time with winds of up to 150 miles (240 km) an hour. The raging gales, torrents of rain and flood tides may sound exciting to an outsider but, in fact, they're terrifying and often tragic.

The most recent hurricane in Florida's history took place on 24 August 1992. The worst storm in 60 years, Hurricane Andrew hit Florida near the small town of Homestead, 30 miles (48 km) south of Miami Beach, then swept across the state and into the Gulf of Mexico. Twenty-seven people were killed and hundreds of millions of dollars' worth of damage was caused. Fortunately, most of the devastation was confined to a relatively small area in the southern part of Dade County. Massive relief efforts, including a huge 'Labor of Love' project organized on America's Labor Day weekend, meant that virtually all of Florida's hotels and attractions were up and running within a few days of the hurricane. Those sights still closed for repairs at the time of writing are listed on p. 35.

Statistically, hurricanes hit Florida only once every seven years, between the months of June and November. Your chance of being in the wrong place at the wrong time is therefore minimal.

Agriculture was expanded to provide winter vegetables for the north and more fruit, especially citrus. Cattle farmers profited from cheap land prices in Florida's interior. The 1959 revolution in Cuba brought an influx of 300,000, swelling Miami's population and adding to growth.

Recent decades have seen the love affair with Florida continue. Jumbo jets bring vacationers in greater numbers than ever. Winter sun seekers drive down the interstate highways from frigid northern cities in just a couple of days.

Travel has yet another dimension in Florida: it was from Cape Canaveral on the Atlantic coast that America first probed into space. Beginning in 1950 with the launch of a modified German V-2, the Cape has seen the blast-off of ever more powerful rockets. From the nearby Kennedy Space Center, American astronauts set out to make man's first landing on the moon in 1969. Today, crowds flock to 'Space Coast' to watch the Space Shuttles lift off on their way to orbit.

Changing Patterns

When Walt Disney quietly started to buy up land near Orlando in the late '60s, he began a process that was to alter Florida tourism beyond recognition. There had long been a handful of purpose-built holiday 'attractions', but Walt Disney World when it opened in 1971 made them look amateur and insignificant. Some rose to the challenge, some went under. Now, Disney World has four times the facilities it opened with and is the most popular vacation destination on earth. Other theme parks cluster around it to get some of the action and Orlando has turned from a sleepy market town to the city with more hotel rooms than any other in the US.

European travellers find Miami and Orlando among the New World's most accessible cities. Refugees from the cold north and the Caribbean still arrive in their thousands. The Spanish explorers sought gold and the fountain of youth. The objectives of today's immigrants and vacationers are not so different.

Where to Go

In terms of size, Florida ranks only 22nd among American states, but at more than 58,000 square miles (150,000 sq. km) it's the size of England and Wales combined. There's enough to see and do to keep you going for months, let alone the average two-week holiday. So you will have to make choices. The Gulf Coast or the Atlantic Coast? Combined with Walt Disney World? Miami and southern Florida as well? Or instead?

Most visitors hire a car. It's the best means of getting around, even if you plan to stay in one area. Rates are economical, fuel is cheap, the roads are good and not too crowded, and it's easy to find your way.

In this book we travel north from Miami up the Atlantic Coast through Fort Lauderdale, Palm Beach and the 'Space Coast' to St Augustine. Then we look at booming Orlando and Central Florida, home of Walt Disney World and several more theme parks before going south to the Everglades and the Florida Keys. Finally, we visit the fast-expanding resorts of the Gulf Coast, travelling north from Naples to Clearwater Beach. But first comes a famous American vacation spot, now in the process of undergoing an exciting revival.

Miami Beach

The city of Miami Beach, 'where the sun spends the winter', is in fact a narrow 7-mile (11-km) strip of land separated from mainland Miami by Biscayne Bay and connected to it by causeways. It's here that you'll find something of the opulence and brash taste that have become as much a part of the American legend as the Wild West.

Collins Avenue, the north-south spine of the island, is lined by hotels and holiday apartments. The resort's heyday was in the 1950s when vast pleasure palaces aspired to be the biggest and most luxurious: 20 years later it was no longer fashionable to be seen at Miami Beach. Now the place has **23**

picked itself up and is being discovered by a new generation. Hotels have had face-lifts, some admittedly superficial. They still try to outdo each other, but except in high season the competition mainly takes the form of offering special rates.

In contrast are the more modest Art Deco hotels and 'Pullmanettes' (compact self-service apartments) of **South Beach**, an area developed in the 1930s and now revitalized. The seafront along **Ocean Drive** benefits from a wide strip of grass and especially between about 10th and 13th Streets it's

become a trendy place to be seen. Real or would-be models and other 'beautiful people' parade or preen themselves at the open-air bars, while bikers and roller skaters cut in and out of the sunset traffic snarl.

The **Bass Museum of Art** (just off Collins Avenue at 21st Street) has a small but select collection including baroque sculpture, Regency portraits, Tibetan and Nepalese bronzes and, appropriately, architectural designs of the 1930s.

The Miami Beach business district, just north of South Beach, includes Lincoln Road

Mall, a pedestrian shopping street. Most of the modestly priced accommodations lie between South Beach and 41st Street. Then, above Arthur Godfrey Boulevard, come the top-of-the-line hotels, including the legendary **Fontainebleau Hilton**. (If you're driving north up Collins Avenue, you'll see a huge mural of the hotel apparently blocking the way.) The 'Fount'n-Blue', as it's usually pronounced, is a resort in itself, with pools, waterfalls, grottoes, hidden bars, shops, a tennis centre and an aquarium. It has been modernized but the memory lingers on of an America now only found on film, when Hollywood stars stayed regularly at the Fontainebleau.

The rambling Miami Beach **boardwalk** begins at 21st Street and runs between the big hotels and the beach, as far as 46th Street. The wooden walkway made a hit when it opened in 1984 with its covered pavilions providing shaded places to sit. The beach is impressively wide and flat, but not especially attractive and quite difficult to reach in places. (Too often in the United States, although the shore itself is mostly open to the public, private property bars the way and there are few points of access.) Around 74th Street you'll again find more modest hotels and a small town feeling.

NORTH OF MIAMI BEACH

Continuing north along the string of offshore islands, Route A1A winds through the pleasant resort of **Surfside** (at about 93rd Street) and then on to **Bal Harbour**, with its waffle-faced condominiums and elegant hotels. Don't miss Bal Harbour Shops, a luxury mall renowned as much for its setting as the merchandise it sells.

Further along A1A **Haulover Park** is sandwiched between the bay and the ocean. On the bay side, Haulover Marina has berths for dozens of fishing boats, and it's the **25**

T he world-famous resort of Miami Beach 'where the sun spends the winter'.

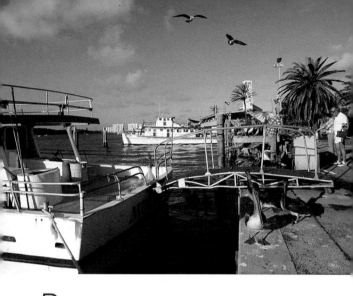

*B*oats moored at Bal Harbour north of Miami Beach.

starting point for cruises along the Intra-Coastal Waterway to Fort Lauderdale. The ocean side of the park has an acceptable family beach with picnic places.

The Sunny Isles (around 167th Street) attract package tour vacationers. You can fish from the pier, dance in the nightclubs and see a cabaret. Close by on the mainland, just

off 167th Street near US 1, you'll come to the tranquil **St Bernard's (or the Old Spanish) Monastery**, billed as 'the oldest building in North America'. In fact, it has only stood here since the early 1950s!

The 12th-century cloisters from Segovia were bought by the press magnate William Randolph Hearst for his estate

The Art Deco District

Thanks to the extraordinary number of buildings in the 'stream-lined modern' style, one square mile (2.6 sq. km) of Miami Beach known as the **Art Deco district** has been declared a national preservation zone. Nowhere else in America is there such a concentration of architecture from the 1930s and early forties. Hotels and apartments were built at modest cost using cast concrete and stucco, decorated with chrome, stainless steel, glass blocks and plastics. Thumbing its nose at the depression, the flashy style set out to attract a new generation of middle class tourists. The Miami Design Preservation League organizes guided tours of this unique quarter (tel. 672-2014). If you walk it on your own, stroll along Ocean Drive between 5th and 15th Streets and the neighbouring blocks to the west.

at San Simeon in California, dismantled and shipped over in 1925. The crates were all numbered, but customs inspectors broke them open and mixed up the stones. Hearst lost interest and it was left to others to reassemble the puzzle.

Around 196th Street, **Aventura** is famous for its exclusive golf and tennis resorts, and for a shopping mall which is vast even by local standards. The resorts continue in an unbroken line to the north, but at this point we turn back to Florida's sprawling metropolis.

Miami

As much a Latin American as a North American city, with as many Spanish-speakers as English, Miami is a fast-moving picture. It was no more than a village when the railroad baron Henry Flagler was persuaded to extend his tracks this far south in 1896. Now the metropolitan population exceeds 3 million and the suburbs stretch for 30 miles (50 km). Some neighbourhoods are on their way up, others are run-down and some are definitely 'no-go' areas.

miles (50 km). Some neighbourhoods are on their way up, others are run-down and some are definitely 'no-go' areas.

The Metrorail elevated railway brings people from the northern and southern suburbs into the city centre, while the automated Metromover makes a loop round the downtown district. A ride on this one is primarily for fun and the views: the system doesn't actually cover much ground. It was built as part of a renewal programme for downtown Miami, which is certainly livelier than it was in the 1970s, although the shops are mostly of the fast-buck variety.

Flagler Street is the main east-west artery and is the 'zero' for Miami's street numbers. Streets run east-west; avenues run north-south with **Miami Avenue** as the 'zero'. In the four quadrants thus created, streets and avenues are labelled NE, SE, SW, and NW.

M*odern skyline of downtown Miami.*

(See map of Miami and Miami Beach on cover flap.)

The **Metro-Dade Cultural Center** (101 West Flagler Street), an arcaded building around a central plaza, was designed in post-modernist style by Philip Johnson. Under one roof are the **Center for the Fine Arts** (an art gallery and sculpture court with space for temporary exhibitions), an auditorium, Miami's central public library and the **Historical Museum of Southern Florida**. The latter features dozens of hands-on displays. You can, for example, set the sails and haul the rigging on an old sailing boat – symbol of Florida's pioneer era.

Biscayne Boulevard, close to the waterfront, doubles as part of the circuit for Miami's Grand Prix and the route of the annual Orange Bowl Parade on New Year's Eve. The **Omni** centre, a huge shopping, entertainment and hotel complex occupies a stretch of Boulevard frontage near the Venetian Causeway to Miami Beach.

Flagler Street meets Biscayne Boulevard and the Bay at Bayfront Park. The big draw **29** here is **Bayside**, a waterfront complex of shops and eating places with its own pier, yacht berths, promenade and free entertainment under the palms. North and across a drawbridge is the **Port of Miami**, home base for sleek cruise ships which sail the Caribbean.

South of Bayfront Park, Du Pont Plaza is a centre of international banking and business with a concentration of

luxury hotels and the 5,000-seat **Miami Convention Center**. Across the Miami River to the south, **Brickell Avenue** is lined with high-rise office buildings and apartment complexes.

While **Little Havana** begins in downtown Miami,

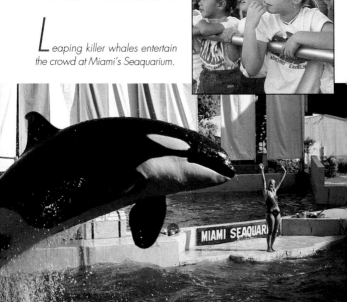

Leaping killer whales entertain the crowd at Miami's Seaquarium.

the centre of the district is a 30-block section stretching west along 8th Street, called *Calle Ocho*. Restaurants here specialize in Cuban and other Latin American cuisine and street-side snack bars serve strong and aromatic *café cubano*. Lots of small businesses flourish in the area, too. It's estimated that over 600,000 Cubans now live in Miami, making them the largest ethnic group.

KEY BISCAYNE

One of the earliest marine parks, the **Seaquarium** is reached by the Rickenbacker Causeway, 'the steepest hill in Miami', where it arcs over the Bay towards the island of Key Biscayne. Compared with Sea World in Orlando, this one is showing its age, but has the merit that you are very close to the action.

Shows are timed so that spectators can move from one performance to the next to see shark-feeding, juggling sea lions, leaping killer whales and basketball-playing dolphins (the 'Miami Heatwave', not to be confused with the local human team, the Miami Heat). These friendly performers live for a long time, but the dolphin named 'Flipper' who stars here is a successor, not the original who had a TV show years ago.

The Seaquarium is one of the few places where you can see the rare manatee or sea-cow, though you might be lucky and spot one in the wild. Large seal-like mammals, they used to live in great numbers in Florida's waterways before the advent of propeller-driven speed boats, which killed many of them.

The northern part of Key Biscayne is given over to **Crandon Park**, a vast public beach with picnic facilities. Don't pick the sea oats that line the beach; they prevent erosion of the sand.

The southern end of the island is the **Bill Baggs State Recreation Area**, site of the 1825 Cape Florida lighthouse. Ask at the entrance gate about tours of the restored keeper's house and the lighthouse itself (closed Tuesdays). The 95-ft (30-m) climb up into **31**

THE 'GABLES' AND THE 'GROVE'

South-west of the city centre, the wealthy community of **Coral Gables** is graced with fountains, tropical gardens and Spanish architecture. The **Lowe Art Museum** on the University of Miami campus (1301 Stanford Drive) has collections of primitive and native American art, 17th-century Spanish paintings and 20th-century art, especially sculpture.

Coconut Grove is a lively village-cum-suburb on the shores of the bay, with cosy little shops, bikeways, open-air cafés, clubs and live theatre. It dates back to the years before Miami existed – a few early buildings still survive, notably **The Barnacle**, built from timber salvaged from shipwrecks.

Down by the sheltered yacht harbour, the little Art Deco building which now serves as **Miami City Hall** started life as the terminal for Pan American's flying boats, which took off from the bay for Cuba and points south in the 1930s. In the late afternoon stroll through the centre of the Grove, watching out for kamikaze rollerbladers slicing through the traffic – but don't stray too far to the west, a deprived and notoriously dangerous area.

At the Miami end of Coconut Grove, the Italianate palace of **Vizcaya** (3251 S. Miami Avenue) was built for the tractor magnate James Deering. An odd but imposing mixture of styles, it is decorated with tapestries, massive furniture and classical sculpture. Outside, elegant terraces sweep down to the bay, but the grounds also include dense jungle, left uncut at Deering's insistence. Follow the detailed Vizcaya guidebook when you tour the house.

Across South Miami Avenue, opposite Vizcaya, the **Museum of Science** features dozens of hands-on exhibits, while the adjacent **Space Transit Planetarium** screens a series of multi-media laser shows highlighting various aspects of astronomy. The adjoining wildlife centre provides a home for injured birds of prey.

SOUTH OF THE CITY

South on Old Cutler Road, the lush **Fairchild Tropical Garden** comprises over 80 acres (32 ha) of tropical plants,

The trendy village of Coconut Grove on the shores of Biscayne Bay.

33

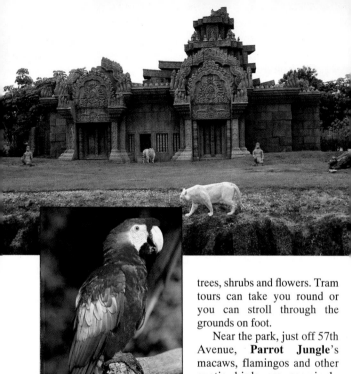

trees, shrubs and flowers. Tram tours can take you round or you can stroll through the grounds on foot.

Near the park, just off 57th Avenue, **Parrot Jungle**'s macaws, flamingos and other exotic birds are seemingly unrestricted. Parrots will eat out of your hand – you can feed them with approved seed dispensed by slot machines. Trained birds ride bicycles, roller-skate and count, while the 'Senior Psittacines', retired parrots of 50 years old and more, doze contentedly on their perches.

Exotic wildlife at the Metrozoo and Parrot Jungle south of Miami.

The Gold Coast

About an hour south of Miami, **Monkey Jungle** (at SW 216th Street) keeps human visitors caged while 500 other primates are free to swing, climb and dive in the cultivated tropical jungle. In the same area, one of the world's largest outdoor orchid gardens can be found at **Orchid Jungle** (26715 SW 157th Avenue).

At least five different roads lead north from Miami along this celebrated 70-mile (112-km) stretch of Atlantic coastline. The older highway US 1 lies just inland from the coast; then comes I-95, the multi-lane Interstate, best if you want to travel fast; the Florida turnpike

---

Warning!

As a result of Hurricane Andrew in August 1992, some of the following attractions may still be closed for repairs at the time of your visit:

1. Metrozoo. 12400 SW 152nd Street. Tel. (305) 251-0400.

2. Gold Coast Railroad Museum. Situated opposite the Metrozoo's main entrance. Tel. (305) 253-0063.

3. Weeks Air Museum. Kendall-Tamiami Airport. Tel. (305) 233-5197.

4. Biscayne National Park. Tel. (305) 247-2400.

5. Everglades National Park. Tel. (305) 247-6211.

Toll-free telephone lines have also been set up to provide up-to-the-minute information regarding the status of each. Numbers to call are listed below.

Australia: 0014-800-126-084.

Canada and the USA: 800-283-2707.

France: 05-90-0998.

United Kingdom: 0800-89-2994.

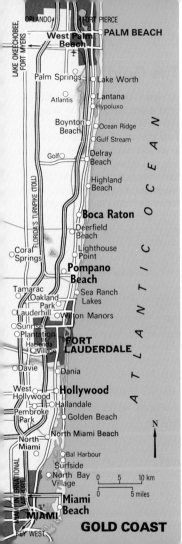

GOLD COAST

toll road and US 441 run further inland than the others. Nearest to the sea is route A1A. For much of the way it links the barrier islands – there are some fabulous views along the way, but the many traffic lights can make it slow going.

This coastline includes half a dozen of Florida's most famous winter resorts, all with wide boulevards, white-painted banks, motels, hotels, condominiums and restaurants. At first glance it's difficult to distinguish one place from another, but they all have enough individuality to inspire loyalty in their regular visitors.

The first rather quiet resorts north of Miami are **Hallandale** and **Hollywood**, more rural at its northern end. They're both favoured by older people, especially Canadians. **Dania**, north-west of Hollywood, is known locally as the antique capital of Florida and all along US 1 dealers have set up shops in the sunshine. Dania also has its own Jai Alai Fronton.

Fort Lauderdale straddles more than 200 miles (320 km) of inland waterways, lined with over 30,000 private boats and yachts. Most hotels and many motels face the beach, separated from it by the coast road. You can park in sight of the waves and make forays to restaurants across the highway.

The best way to get acquainted with the town is to ride one of the rubber-wheeled sightseeing 'trams'. Guides give commentaries as the tour passes sumptuous waterfront homes, the car museum, orange groves, and the Seminole Village, where you can see alligator wrestling or play bingo for high stakes. (The self-administering Seminole nation can bypass state laws on gambling.)

For a complete change of scene, visit the **Museum of Art** (1 E. Las Olas Boulevard) with its strong, emphatically modern art and various ethnographic collections.

Ocean World on SE 17th Street entertains visitors with its dolphin and sea lion shows, tanks of sharks, turtles, reef fish and alligators, caged monkeys and macaws.

Across the street from Ocean World, the misleadingly named Port Everglades is a major terminal for cruise ships and freighters. All sorts of **cruises** start from Fort Lauderdale, some going as far as the Bahamas. Mississippi-style paddle-boats take daytime trips to the mangrove swamps and dinner cruises along the Intra-Coastal Waterway.

North from Fort Lauderdale, **Pompano Beach** is lined with towering condominiums, and well known for the trotting races held at Pompano Park. Expensive parking keeps the beach quieter at **Boca Raton**, where as many people fish from the shore as take to the water. Boca claims to be the 'Winter Polo Capital of the World'. The sport is played on Sundays between January and April.

North past the apartments and golf clubs of Delray Beach brings you to **Lake Worth**. Casino Park Beach, a stretch of sloping sand next to Kreusler Memorial Park, sometimes has good waves for surfing. The **Museum of Art** (601 Lake Avenue) houses ultra-modern exhibitions in a converted Art Deco cinema.

37

Palm Beach to St Augustine

PALM BEACH

Beautiful Italianate homes are half hidden behind walls and sculptured hedges here, in one of America's wealthiest communities. Some of the houses crowded along the five-mile (8-km) strip of land are used only for a few weeks each winter, while the rest of the year they lie empty. Others may be rented to tourists. Drive along A1A to admire the landscape gardening and see how the seriously rich arrange things when they get the chance. From Christmas to the end of February it's hard to park, or even to stop; at other times Palm Beach can be very quiet. The beach itself is narrow, since storms have eroded much of it away.

For another glimpse of the good life, stroll along glamorous **Worth Avenue** amid Mediterranean-style buildings from the 1920s with palm-filled courtyards, elegant shops and restaurants. It all makes Beverly Hills' Rodeo Drive look comparatively down-market. Plays straight from Broadway come to spend the winter at the Royal Poinciana Playhouse.

The **Henry Morrison Flagler Museum** on Cocoanut Row, formerly the rail tycoon's extravagant 1901 mansion known as 'Whitehall', retains some original furniture and photographs. Flagler's own railway carriage is parked in the garden, complete with copper-lined shower and cast-iron stove.

Across the causeway, **West Palm Beach** has the motels, businesses, light industry and international airport which its well-groomed neighbour wasn't prepared to accommodate. The **Norton Gallery of Art** on US 1 (1451 S. Olive Avenue) has a splendid collection of French impressionists and post-impressionists, including Gauguin's *The Agony in the Garden* and some fine Chinese jade.

From West Palm Beach, the causeway at Blue Heron Boulevard leads across to Palm Beach Shores, a new development of hotels and motels with a variety of leisure facilities.

Inland at **Lion Country Safari** you can drive through herds of elephants and zebras, past lions and ostriches. If you come in a convertible, you'll have to swap it for one of the park's cars.

The area labelled the Gold Coast ends at West Palm Beach. Under different names (Treasure Coast, Space Coast and First Coast), the Florida beaches continue for another 300 miles (480 km) to the state border.

Treasure Coast acquired its name from the Spanish ships which were wrecked along it, spilling their cargoes of gold and silver. (But truth to tell, any part of Florida's Atlantic seaboard could make the same claim.) Once a mangrove swamp with offshore sandbars, much of it is a long string of islands separated from the mainland by a saltwater strip called Indian River or Indian Creek. The leisurely route A1A connects the islands and resorts, frequently crossing bridges where Indian River is linked to the ocean by inlets.

Travelling in style: the railway tycoon's own personal car.

39

The **Jonathan Dickenson State Park**, 13 miles (20 km) south of Stuart, provides vacation cabins, hookups for campers and facilities for fishing, swimming, boating, canoeing and hiking. **Jupiter Beach** to the south and Jupiter Island to the north are largely unbuilt-up and there's plenty of free parking. Between Fort Pierce and Melbourne, sand dunes, shell shops, motels and the occasional steakhouse are the main features of the landscape.

SPACE COAST

A nature reserve with alligators, eagles and armadillos shares **Merritt Island** with scented orange groves and with NASA (the National Aeronautics and Space Administration). Here, at Cape Canaveral, the United States began to send rockets into space in the 1950s.

Nearby, the **John F. Kennedy Space Center** has been the launch site for American manned exploration of space, including the first mission to land a man on the moon in 1969. Now it's the base of

The multi-stage Saturn launcher at JFK Space Center.

the Space Shuttles. To find out when the next take-off is scheduled, check the daily papers or call 1-800-432-2153. Whether there's a launch or not, it's well worth visiting the Spaceport, just off NASA Causeway linking A1A and US 1. Expect to spend at least half a day.

The 'Rocket Garden' includes the kind of launchers that put the first Americans into space and it's remarkable how small they look now. The **Astronauts' Memorial** honours those killed in the space programme. An appropriate blend of technology and sculpture, it turns with the sun and reflects light behind their names. Multimedia shows and exhibits explain the amazing technology of space travel, and a small lump of real moon rock is on show.

On the **Red Bus Tour** (which may vary for operational reasons), you'll be shown the highlights of the moon landing programme. This includes the gigantic 520-ft (158-m) VAB (Vehicle Assembly Building), a huge Saturn moon rocket, the moon launch pad and Mission Control. The Blue Bus Tour is more for rocket buffs – it deals with the unmanned programme. The **IMAX films** shown on five-storey high screens are thrilling: *The Dream is Alive*, also shown at the Air & Space Museum in Washington DC, is the story of the Space Shuttle; *Blue Planet* is a riveting geography lesson. Allow at least half a day for a visit.

East of the Spaceport, Port Canaveral is the newest of Florida's cruise terminals. If your holiday combines Orlando with a cruise, your ship will probably leave from here.

Cocoa Beach, on the narrow island strip to the south, was tiny when the first astronauts came here to relax from their training. Now it's a growing resort, a favourite among surfers and teenagers who jam its sands near the old wooden pier. The dunes are a great vantage point for watching space launches. **41**

Some 50 miles (80 km) north of Cape Canaveral near New Smyrna Beach is the inlet where Ponce de León, credited as the discoverer of Florida, stepped ashore in 1513.

Then comes the 'World's Most Famous Beach', as **Daytona Beach** proudly proclaims itself. Its 23 miles (37 km) of hard-packed sand doubles as a roadway for a $3 toll, although every so often a stalled car gets caught by the tide. The 10 mph (16 kph) limit hardly recalls the roaring twenties and thirties when Sir Henry Segrave and Sir Malcolm Campbell set world land speed records here, culminating in Campbell's 276 mph (444 kph) in 1935.

The flat sands, lifeguard towers and shallow water make it safe for children. And like every Florida beach, it's most perfect at dawn, when early joggers scarcely bother the myriad sea birds and waders.

On 4 July each year, the annual 400-mile (645-km) stock-car race is held at the **Daytona International Speedway**. The Daytona 500 is usually scheduled for late February. An entire car and motorcycle culture has grown up around the

Last Fling for Old Hardware

When President Kennedy declared in 1961 that the US would put a man on the moon (and bring him back) before the decade was out, no one knew how it could be achieved. Everything had to be designed and built from scratch. What is so striking now, apart from the colossal size of the multi-stage Saturn launcher and the sheer daring of those who rode on its nose, is the old-fashioned 'nuts and bolts' appearance of it all. It looks like World War II equipment and with reason. The engineers were taking enough chances as it was, so they built what they knew. Despite today's vaunted technology, one has to wonder if the will, the courage and the money could be summoned up to do the job now or ever again.

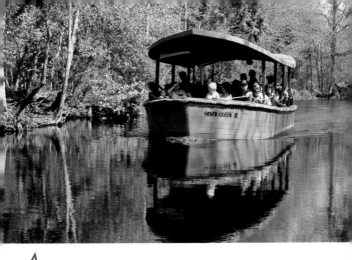

A safari boat cruises through primeval jungle in Silver Springs.

track with parades, flea markets and special events. Hot rodders and bikers in black leather cruise the streets and burn rubber at the traffic lights.

INLAND EXCURSION

A trip to Lake George and Ocala National Forest is worth the drive westwards from Ormond Beach. Off Highway 40 at Juniper Springs, warm clear water surges out of the ground to form a natural swimming pool. There are other spa-resorts, notably Alexander Springs to the south of the forest and **Silver Springs** on its western edge. Here you can view a menagerie of animals from a safari boat, or spot fish and underwater plants through the floor of a glass-bottomed boat. Elsewhere on the grounds are a reptile institute, waterslides and a collection of antique cars.

Route 19 through the **Ocala National Forest**, itself a sizable **43** wilderness of lakes, hills and springs, offers first-class camping, hiking and fishing. To the west is the town of Ocala and 35 miles (56 km) to the north-west, the university city of Gainsville.

First Coast is the label given to the northern end of Florida's Atlantic seaboard, site of the earliest European settlements in the region. Dolphins and whales leaping and cavorting in the water can be seen at **Marineland**, where the idea of sea-life parks began. Dating from the 1930s, it grew into a resort but the buildings are now showing their age and newer parks have left it behind.

*D*olphins perform spectacular acrobatics at Marineland.

ST AUGUSTINE

You'll come to shrug off superlatives in Florida, but this really *is* the oldest city in the United States (founded in 1565, long before the *Mayflower*). Its Spanish architecture, churches and distinctly colonial atmosphere make it unlike anywhere else in Florida.

Most striking of the buildings is the **Castillo de San Marcos**, a star-shaped Spanish fortress started in 1672 as a response to repeated raids by pirates and the English (in some cases there was no clear distinction between the two categories). Completed in 1695, its fortified walls are up to 12 ft (3.7 m) thick in places, built of *coquina*, a stone formed

The 19th-century Ponce de León hotel in St Augustine, built by railway baron Henry Flagler.

of naturally bonded seashells and so effective at absorbing bombardment that the fortress never fell to assault. Exhibits and recreations of the historical events connected with the fort are presented daily. (See p. 134.)

A sightseeing road-train will take you on a tour of the historic old city, and then you can return to landmarks such as the well-restored **Oldest House** or the **Oldest Store Museum**. This turn-of-the-century emporium is stocked with 100,000 authentic items from that period, many of them accidentally discovered in a warehouse attic. You can see old buttoned shoes and lace corsets, toys, groceries, medicines, bonnets, bicycles, hats and guns.

Henry Flagler built the imposing Ponce de León Hotel **45**

for the new wave of tourists when his railroad reached St Augustine in 1888. Now, it houses Flagler College. If you can, take a look inside the rotunda, the former hotel lobby. Outside again, notice the early use of poured concrete, strangely allied with such decorative architecture. Across the street, another Flagler hotel is now the **Lightner Museum**, a collection of Victoriana, Tiffany glass and 19th-century musical instruments. A third former hotel on the square makes an impressive City Hall. On summer evenings at the St Augustine amphitheatre, the city's founding is re-enacted in an outdoor pageant, 'Cross and Sword'.

Orlando and Central Florida

Now the largest city in central Florida, **Orlando** entered the tourist business in a big way when Walt Disney World moved in down the road. The huge number of hotel rooms in the area now means that Orlando can accommodate the biggest conventions and sports events, and a flow of visitors packs the city. Central Florida offers the world's greatest collection of purpose-built attractions.

Many visitors to the area stay at or near Disney World or on International Drive, and never venture into downtown Orlando, which is a pity. It's hard to tell what has been restored and what is brand-new at **Church Street Station**, a complex of fun shopping, food and entertainment. It's all open during the day, but after about 5.30 p.m. you have to pay to get in. There may be a dozen shows to choose from – ranging from jazz bands to cancan girls to elegant Country and Western opera across the street at the Cheyenne Saloon. (The gambling here is only 'pretend'.) Street entertainers, pubs and restaurants add to the downtown diversions.

International Drive, 12 miles (19 km) away and as far again from Disney World, has grown from nothing in just a few years. Entirely a creation of the tourist boom, it's a glitzy strip of hotels, fast-food outlets, bars and all-you-can-eat buffets.

In the years before Disney, **Kissimmee** was a sleepy town where the local cattle ranchers might drop in once a week. Now, it's hard to find the old centre, amid miles and miles of motels, T-shirt 'factory outlets' and 'British' pubs. If you persist, you'll find it along Main Street and Broadway, where nothing much has changed. The town still holds a cattle market, and a rodeo twice a year.

The **Flying Tigers Warbirds Air Museum** at the local airport has a collection of rare old planes in various stages of restoration. You can take a flight in an open biplane or the airship which you'll see cruising overhead when you're in the theme parks.

Flavour of the Wild West at the Cheyenne Saloon in Orlando.

Walt Disney World

Tens of millions of people come every year to Walt Disney World, the most popular tourist attraction on earth, lying 20 miles (32 km) southwest of Orlando off Interstate 4 and US 192. It's not just one theme park, but three, and an immense holiday resort with dozens of hotels, a campground, five golf courses, aquaparks, tennis courts, vacation villas and shops. Statistics show that 80% of visitors are adults, although for the purposes of Disney ticket sales, adulthood begins at the age of 10. Disney World has even become America's favourite honeymoon destination. In all, the site covers some 28,000 acres (11,000 ha), roughly twice the area of Manhattan Island.

Visitors to Disney World generally divide their time between the **Magic Kingdom**, the **Disney-MGM Studios** and the nearby **EPCOT Center**. A day for each is hardly enough, and if you stay longer, there are still more major attractions within the Disney area, including Typhoon Lagoon and River Country (water adventure parks) and Pleasure Island (bars, nightclubs and live entertainment). To encourage you, there are money-saving 4-day and 5-day passes as well as one-day, one park tickets. (See p. 136 for approximate prices. They may seem expensive, but once inside, all rides and attractions are free.) Several tour companies operate excursions – travel agents can give you details of what's available.

THE MAGIC KINGDOM

From the Ticket and Transportation Center, take the sleek monorail or a ferryboat across the lake. (Buses for Disney hotel guests go straight to the entrance.) The Magic Kingdom is divided into seven different 'lands'. Stroll from one to the next but not too slowly – there's a lot to see and do.

Main Street USA. Just beyond the entrance, you pass beneath Main Street Railroad Station into Town Square. **City Hall**, to your left, is the place for information about any aspect of Disney World. The square is always filled with life, and sometimes a crowd clustering round one of the Disney characters (they'll sign autographs but they don't speak).

Ahead of you, buildings in early 20th-century style line Main Street. Soon you'll see an antique double-decker bus or horse-drawn tram. You'll want to stop at the shops, but try to be at the other end by 9 a.m. when the other lands open.

At the end of the street and across a bridge, a circular **Plaza** is backed by **Cinderella Castle**, the pinnacled symbol of the Magic Kingdom. Radial routes lead to all the 'lands'. Our description proceeds clockwise but don't follow any formula too strictly. Pick out things that appeal to you.

Adventureland. First you'll spot the giant banyan tree which supports the Swiss Family Treehouse. For all its woody appearance, it's actually made of concrete and vinyl. Just beyond you can board boats for the **Jungle Cruise** or join **Pirates of the Caribbean**

for a voyage to their treasure trove.

Frontierland celebrates America's Old West, both real and legendary. Take aim at the old-time Shootin' Gallery, go for a roller-coaster ride through Gold Rush days on the **Big Thunder Mountain Railroad**, board an elegant triple-decker or raft across to Tom Sawyer Island. The **Diamond Horseshoe Jamboree** is a live show in Wild West style. (Book seats at the Disneyana Collectibles store in Town Square.) Newest and most popular of the rides here is **Splash Mountain**. Your boat will seem to hang interminably in space before dropping five storeys into a pool.

Liberty Square. A few steps away, the architecture changes from Old West to New England. The **Hall of Presidents** is a major attraction, with America's leaders brought to life through *Audio-Animatronics*. Even though you know the performers are mechanical replicas, the moment will come when you'll feel you're listening to Washington and Lincoln. The **Haunted Mansion** nearby **49**

is more funny than frightening, even when one of its 999 ghosts comes to sit next to you.

Fantasyland. The Magic Kingdom is fantasy throughout, but here it's in the purest form. The **Mad Tea Party** is a good place to begin, with a dizzying whirl in a gigantic teacup. **It's a Small World** sets everyone smiling as they cruise past singing, dancing dolls. Small children adore **Dumbo the Flying Elephant** and **Cinderella's Golden Carrousel**, a classic merry-go-round.

From Fantasyland, you can take the **Skyway** cable car to Tomorrowland or walk through Cinderella Castle past fine mosaics of scenes from the Disney film *Cinderella*.

Mickey's Starland. Newest of the lands, this one is tucked away so you could easily miss it. Mickey's House is set up like a museum of memorabilia but at **Mickey's Hollywood Theater** the Mouse himself is found in his dressing room, ready to sign autographs and pose for pictures.

Tomorrowland is dominated by a white cone of steel, the famous **Space Mountain**. Inside, a thrilling roller-coaster ride races through inky blackness. Be sure to heed the warning signs, and don't attempt the ride if you've got a weak neck, back, heart or stomach. A less nerve-frazzling option is the **WEDWay PeopleMover**, where little cars float on an electromagnetic cushion.

Dreamflight traces aviation's history and in **Grand Prix Cars** you can control the speed, but guide rails stop the race turning into chaos.

Before leaving the Magic Kingdom, take a trip round its borders on the **Walt Disney World Railroad**. The four narrow-gauge steam locomotives which haul the open passenger cars are the real thing. Built in Philadelphia between 1916–28, they were discovered, still hard at work, in Mexico's Yucatan Peninsula in the 1960s.

The fairy-tale wonders of Walt Disney World.

EPCOT CENTER

Twenty years in planning and opened in 1982, Walt Disney World's 'Experimental Prototype Community of Tomorrow' is a park full of attractions to enlighten and entertain with all manner of special effects and computerized gadgetry.

The park has two distinct theme areas, together forming a figure 8. In the first, **Future World**, the pavilions are sponsored by some of America's biggest corporations such as General Motors, Exxon and **51**

Kodak. The second, **World Showcase**, celebrates the cultures and products of eleven different nations. EPCOT is reached by car and shuttle bus and from the Magic Kingdom by monorail.

FUTURE WORLD

The great white sphere near the main entrance is **Spaceship Earth**, symbol of EPCOT. In-side it, a spectacular ride spirals up through scenes depicting the development of communications. Near its base, **Earth Station** is an information centre.

Straight ahead lie the twin buildings of **Communicore, East and West**, where exhibits expand on the communications theme. You can look behind the scenes at the role of computers in Disney World operations. Grouped around Communicore

---

Tips for Touring Disney World

1. Pick your parks. If it's your first visit and you have three days or more, leave the Magic Kingdom for the second or third. If you have only one, choose the Magic Kingdom which is the essence of Disney's fantasy.

2. **Arrive early** to get your money's worth and beat the crowd to the most popular rides. The official opening time is 9 a.m., but Main Street USA is open at 8 a.m. and EPCOT and Disney-MGM Studios open their gates at about 8.30 a.m.

3. Make a note of where you leave your car in the huge parks.

4. Pick up a **free guidebook and map**, and an entertainment schedule and plan a route.

5. Rides last 5 to 15 minutes or so. Access is cleverly controlled, and huge numbers of people can be accommodated 3,000 an hour or more on some rides. The wait time is predicted on signs or by the hosts. You may avoid some lines by starting with rides more distant from the entrance and working back.

are the main attractions of Future World. We take a clockwise route, but you'll need to be flexible depending on the length of the queues.

The **Universe of Energy** show is presented in a travelling theatre; the seats actually move, powered in part by solar cells on the roof of the building. A spectacular film about energy sources is followed by a trip through scenes dramatizing the formation of fossil fuels, complete with dinosaurs and primeval mist.

The **Wonders of Life** include the hilarious *Cranium Command*, putting you inside the head of a boy as he faces the crises of a school day. *The Making of Me*, a funny but serious film, illustrates human reproduction and birth. There's always a rush to *Body Wars*, a thrilling flight simulator ride where you're 'shrunk' and sent rushing through arteries, veins, heart and lungs.

Horizons takes a voyage into the future. **Destinations** include a farm where robots harvest crops and colonies under the sea and in space.

The **World of Motion**, in a suitably wheel-shaped building, takes you on a ride through the history of transport from cave-dwellers, past old coaches and cars to the city of tomorrow.

Journey into Imagination goes on a whimsical journey through the creative process in the company of a couple of characters called Dreamfinder and Figment. In the same pavilion *Captain EO*, a 3-D space adventure film, stars Michael Jackson. The effects are electrifying (and might scare small children).

The Land focusses on food and other useful crops. In *Listen to the Land* you cruise by boat past experimental fish farms and through greenhouses where plants grow in sand or suspended in air. If you are specially interested, sign up for a 45-minute walking tour.

The Living Seas exhibit features an underwater ride to the biggest artificial coral reef in the world, stocked with marine life from dolphins to barracuda. In the Coral Reef restaurant, you can dine alongside these underwater wonders. **53**

WORLD SHOWCASE

Ranged round the perimeter of a lagoon stand replicas of some of the world's great monuments. A scale model of the Eiffel Tower rises above the Florida landscape; a diminutive version of Venice's Campanile stands near a Mayan pyramid from Mexico, and so on. Eleven nations are represented, all with restaurants featuring the national cuisine.

Mexico's pyramid houses priceless pre-Colombian treasures and a river-boat trip through Mexican history.

Norway offers a boat trip too on the stormy *Maelstrom*. The Akershus restaurant puts on a typical Norwegian buffet.

China's circular Temple of Heaven is just right for the film *Wonders of China*.

Germany concentrates on traditional food and beer, and shops selling fine glass, silver, porcelain, chocolates and wine.

Italy too emphasizes eating and drinking, in a branch of L'Originale Alfredo di Roma. Street performers entertain the crowds in 'St Mark's Square'.

The United States takes centre stage. *The American Adventure* takes a half-hour journey through American history, in film and special effects including some of the most life-like *Audio-Animatronics* figures yet made by Disney.

Japan shows a formal face, with tranquil gardens and temples. Four eating places serve Japanese dishes, and there's a branch of a famous Tokyo department store.

Morocco's authentic buildings are a World Showcase highlight. They house a colourful bazaar and the Restaurant Marrakesh, where a belly dancer diverts the diners.

France concentrates on gastronomy in three French restaurants with an all-French staff. Don't miss the big-screen film *Impressions de France*.

The United Kingdom cultivates an 'olde worlde' image with Tudor buildings and the Rose and Crown Pub and Dining Room.

Canada shows a Circle-Vision 360 film and Inuit (Eskimo) and Indian crafts are a special feature in the shops.

DISNEY-MGM STUDIOS

Celebrating the American love affair with 'the movies', the newest of the Disney World theme parks opened in 1989, a mile south-west of EPCOT. They really do make films and TV programmes here, but above all it's fun. The streets are full of all kinds of happenings and surprises, so here we mention only some of the highlights.

Inside the entrance, leave the shops until later and walk down **Hollywood Boulevard** towards the big open space of Sunset Plaza. On the right you'll see a giant **clapperboard** chalked with all the latest information on shows and waiting times. Nearby, the open-air **Theater of the Stars** stages a live musical based on Disney's hit *Beauty and the Beast*.

Many who arrive as the gates open run to a ride or show which will have long lines later. Here, they head for **Star Tours**, a simulator thrill created by George Lucas in the tradition of *Star Wars*. On an imaginary but all too convincing trip to Endor, you're thrown around while a synchronized 70-mm film shows the frightening view from the out-of-control spacecraft. Then, those in the know head straight for the **Indiana Jones Stunt Spectacular**. The name says it all.

In **The Great Movie Ride**, your seats carry you

*C*heck the daily attractions at Disney-MGM Studios.

through animated scenes from *Casablanca*, *The Wizard of Oz*, *Alien* and a dozen more landmark films. Disney-MGM is now the official home of **The Muppets**, the late Jim Henson's inspired creations, and you can see them 'on set' in the street or in a remarkable 3-D film. **Voyage of the Little Mermaid** is a multi-media show based on the Disney film – be prepared to get splashed!

The Backstage Tours shouldn't be missed. **Studio Tour** takes you on a shuttle ride past costuming, scene-building and props departments. Next, **Catastrophe Canyon** is where 'by mistake' you get mixed up in a disaster movie complete with earthquake, explosions, fires and a flash flood. When you've recovered, you can walk through the **Special Effects and Production Tour**. Before 5 p.m. or so, when the artists pack up work for the day, go to **The Magic of Disney Animation** for a walking tour which will give you an insight into the intricate process by which animated films are made.

PLEASURE ISLAND

Conscious that they were losing guests in the evenings to the attractions of downtown Orlando and elsewhere, the Disney organization decided to create some nightlife of its own. This is the result, a complex of bars and dance halls, a Comedy Warehouse, clubs and live bands on an open-air stage. The setting is the abandoned, ramshackle old warehouses of some run-down port all specially built in 1989. There's an entrance fee in the evening, but it's free during the day.

MORE ATTRACTIONS AT WALT DISNEY WORLD

Typhoon Lagoon is a giant aquapark with sandy beaches, waterslides and gentle streams where you can drift along sitting in a rubber ring. Its claim to fame, though, is a huge lagoon where the world's biggest wave-making machine generates mighty rollers up to six ft (1.8 m) high for body-surfing.

The older **River Country** has more waterslides, a lakeside beach, white-water rapids, and ropes and bridges for swinging and dropping into the 'old swimming hole'.

Across the water from here, **Discovery Island** is a nature sanctuary with boardwalks meandering past the exotic plant and bird life. They've had some signal successes here with the breeding of endangered species.

For more information about Disney events, accommodation, prices and packages, contact Walt Disney World, Box 10,000, Lake Buena Vista, FL 32830. Tel. (305) 824-4321.

Other Theme Parks in Central Florida

UNIVERSAL STUDIOS

Over 400 acres (160 ha) of realistic sets – San Francisco waterfront, New York streets, Hollywood – and real production equipment make this the biggest facility of its kind east of California. Arrive early if

Confronting the jaws of death at Universal Studios.

you can, collect a map at the gate and plan a route.

Inevitably, when it opened in 1990 comparisons were made with Disney-MGM Studios. Universal tends to be less whimsical, perhaps appealing more to teenagers and film buffs than small children, though even they can't get **57** enough of Yogi Bear and Fred Flintstone in **The Funtastic World of Hanna-Barbera**. Because the area is a lot bigger, the streets may be less crowded and at times it can seem there is less going on. But Universal Studios can claim three of the most thrilling rides anywhere. In **Kongfrontation**, the mighty King Kong, five storeys high, has escaped and is rampaging through New York. You are riding a cable car above a city street when Kong attacks…

Earthquake puts you in a San Francisco subway train, standing peacefully at a station when all hell breaks loose – the effects have actually been measured at 8.3 on the Richter scale. The roof collapses, a truck rolls straight at you, water floods in. It's a relief when the director finally shouts 'Cut!'

'Virtual reality' takes a great leap forward in **Back to the Future**, a ride vaguely based on the films of that name.

*F*lamingos are one of Florida's native species.

You chase through space while an advanced flight simulator convinces you that you're diving out of control, backed by the evidence of amazing images on the huge wrap-around screen.

A Wild West stunt show, adventures based on *ET* and *Ghostbusters*, Alfred Hitchcock's secrets, lessons on gruesome make-up and a backlot 'tram tour' provide more than enough to fill a day.

Sea World, close to International Drive, is the leader in Florida's marine parks. They'll give you a map and an up-to-date schedule of events, specially printed out as you enter, so you can plan your visit. Check the times of the shows: highlights include performing dolphins and sea lions; Shamu the friendly killer whale, propelling a trainer out of the water like a Polaris missile; and water-skiing displays. Between times, visit the seals, or the penguins in their great glass-sided tank refrigerated to the sort of chill they prefer.

In one remarkable exhibit, 'Terrors of the Deep', you walk through a tank full of sharks in a transparent tunnel. Sea World claims to have 'more of everything', including Polynesian dancers, Chinese acrobats and several restaurants. The ride to the top of the 400-ft (120-m) Sky Tower costs a little extra, but is worth it for the view.

On a scorching day, you can cool off at **Wet 'n' Wild** off International Drive (it's closed in winter and bad weather). This collection of lakes and pools is equipped with water-slides, rapids, a wave machine and other sports facilities.

At **Gatorland** (14501 S. Orange Blossom Trial, Kissimmee) they've trained the inmates to 'jump' (actually to push themselves up on their tails) for food. It may seem bizarre, but you can buy deep-fried alligator pieces as a snack, thus eating the cast while you watch the show. This is a big commercial farm too: the shop sells 'gator skin wallets and handbags.

CYPRESS GARDENS

South of Orlando, near Winter Haven, this lakeside park began **59** as a botanic garden in the 1930s. Now it's more famous for the spectacular daily shows on the lake by water-skiers performing acrobatics and forming human pyramids. On shore, Southern Crossroads is a replica of an old southern town (circa 1900) with shops and restaurants. You can ride an electric boat or stroll through the remarkable gardens, home to 8000 species of plants. The 153-ft-high (46-m) Kodak Island in the Sky raises and lowers its passengers every few minutes.

Nearby **Lake Wales** offers a winter home for the North Dakota Black Hills Passion Play. From February to April each year, the huge cast performs the last seven days in the life of Christ in an amphitheatre two miles out of town. The **Bok Singing Tower** is an elegant belfry blending gothic and Art Nouveau, set in quiet gardens on Central Florida's highest hill. Every day at 3 p.m. the resident musician plays a recital on the 57-bell carillon. If you miss it there's a short recorded excerpt every 30 minutes.

The Everglades

Called 'the river of grass' by the Indians, this watery plain is the most famous swamp in the world. Not quite flat, its waters flow almost imperceptibly from Lake Okeechobee south and west into Florida Bay.

The huge 1,400,000-acre (560,000-ha) **Everglades National Park** is a protected area of marshy land and broken coastline. Winter, the dry season, is the ideal time to visit. You'll see most bird life then and there are fewer mosquitoes. For maps and literature, write to Everglades National Park, PO Box 279, Homestead, FL 33030.

Please note that at the time of writing, Everglades National Park was temporarily closed due to the damage caused by Hurricane Andrew. See pp. 21 and 35 for further details.

From Miami head south to Homestead, then take state road 27 and watch for signs to the park. Soon you'll come to the park entrance station, where you can pick up an excellent free map. The park road winds for 38 miles (61 km) to the coast. Several marked turn-offs along the way take you to campsites and picnic grounds beside lakes or near 'hammocks' – raised, usually wooded areas in the swamps.

The first turnoff leads to the **Royal Palm Visitor Center**, on the edge of a freshwater slough (pronounced slew). Look down into the clear waters of the pond to see shoals of fish, including the Florida garfish, one of the principal foods of the alligator. There are brief slide-shows on the Everglades, and the resident rangers will suggest where you should go. The Anhinga Trail's boardwalk circles over the saw-grass marsh. Look for alligators, egrets, herons and the anhinga,

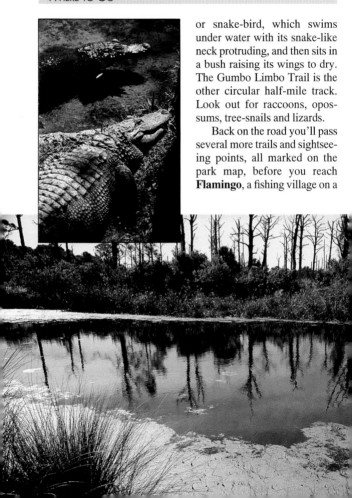

or snake-bird, which swims under water with its snake-like neck protruding, and then sits in a bush raising its wings to dry. The Gumbo Limbo Trail is the other circular half-mile track. Look out for raccoons, opossums, tree-snails and lizards.

Back on the road you'll pass several more trails and sightseeing points, all marked on the park map, before you reach **Flamingo**, a fishing village on a shallow bay, with a colourful history of illicit liquor ('moonshine') production. Now life revolves around a ranger station, a lodge, a campground, restaurant and grocery store. At Flamingo Marina you can buy bait, rent tackle, boats and canoes.

Sightseeing boats take trips from Flamingo, and canoeists find their own way up to Everglades City through a chain of lakes and rivers called 'The Wilderness Waterway'. Look out for great white herons, snowy egrets, roseate spoonbills, ospreys and southern bald eagles. Take plenty of insect repellent, especially in summer. Hunting and firearms are banned, but fishing is permitted.

Another entrance to the park lies off the Tamiami Trail (US 41) which crosses the state from Miami to Naples. Signs all along the Trail promote them, but Coopertown is the centre for **airboat rides**. Flat-bottomed boats, powered by aeroplane propellers will take you sliding over swamp and shooting between clumps of sawgrass. (Airboats are banned in the National Park.)

At the **Miccosukee Indian Village** you can see crafts demonstrations and some rather uninspiring alligator wrestling. The Miccosukee have lived in isolation here since the time of the Seminole wars but fewer than 100 were

*A*lligator-infested swamps in the Florida Everglades. **63**

*T*raditional Indian craftwork at the Miccosukee Village in Everglades National Park.

left when the US government recognized the tribe in 1962. Now there are over 500. Beyond the village, the Tamiami Trail passes along the southern perimeter of the Big Cypress National Preserve.

The western gateway to the National Park is **Everglades City**, the site of another ranger station where you can take leisurely cruises among the '10,000 islands', spotting wildlife. This is still one of the world's largest remaining areas of mangrove forest, although seriously depleted. Preserving what remains is not just conservation for the sake of it: this environment is essential as the breeding ground of commercially important species of fish.

A Selection of Florida Hotels and Restaurants

Recommended Hotels

Long-established and still growing as a holiday destination, Florida offers a huge choice of accommodations. All resorts have representatives of the big chains and franchises, as well as rows of budget motels. The Orlando area, including Walt Disney World, has more hotel rooms than any city in the United States. Competition in the highly developed hospitality industry means that you'll be assured of value for money, whether you choose the most luxurious resort, a modest motel or something in between. Here, we can only make a small selection. We have sub-divided the list by area, following the same order as the Where to Go section of this guide. Each entry is marked with a symbol indicating the price range, per night, for a double room with bath, excluding breakfast. Sales tax of about 6% is added to hotel bills.

In the US, rates quoted are for the room, not per person. Additional occupants over two may be charged a small premium. A few places include a simple continental breakfast. Always ask about special rate packages, e.g. for stays of a few days, lower midweek rates and off-season rates. (Two symbols, e.g. ‖/‖‖ indicate major seasonal variations between prices ranges.)

‖	up to $60
‖‖	$60–$100
‖‖‖	$100–$180
‖‖‖‖	$180 and over

MIAMI BEACH TO AVENTURA

The Alexander |||||
5225 Collins Avenue
Miami Beach, FL 33140
Tel. (305) 865-6500, fax 864-8525
All-suite luxury in pink tower near its own wide beach. Landscaped gardens and pools. 211 rooms.

Colony ||
736 Ocean Drive
Miami Beach, FL 33139
Tel. (305) 673-0088, fax 532-0762
Art-Deco treasure, restored and now a focus of fashionable South Beach. 36 rooms.

Doral Ocean Beach Resort |||
4833 Collins Avenue
Miami Beach, FL 33140
Tel. (305) 532-3600, fax 532-2334
Tower on the ocean. Comprehensive fitness facilities, tennis, pool, boating, golf nearby. 420 rooms.

Edison ||
960 Ocean Drive
Miami Beach, FL 33139
Tel. (305) 531-0461, fax 532-2224
Facing the grass and the sands, in the heart of the trendiest part of South Beach. Restored Art Deco glitter. 82 rooms.

Fontainebleau Hilton |||/||||
4441 Collins Avenue
Miami Beach, FL 33140
Tel. (305) 538-20, fax 534-7821
Huge white curving blocks in lush grounds next to the beach. Pools, tennis. 1206 rooms.

Sheraton Bal Harbour |||/||||
9701 Collins Avenue
Bal Harbour, FL 33154
Tel. (305) 865-7511, fax 864-2601
Landscaped resort on the ocean. Tennis, pools, golf. 650 rooms.

Turnberry Isle Yacht & Country Club ||||
1999 W. Country Club Drive
Aventura, FL 33180
Tel. (305) 932-6200, fax 937-0528
Elegant resort with ocean club, pools, golf courses. 357 rooms.

MIAMI AND AREA

Doubletree ||
2649 S. Bayshore Drive
Coconut Grove, FL 33133
Tel. (305) 858-2500, fax 858-5776
Spacious rooms with views of the bay and the 'Grove'. Pool, tennis. 190 rooms.

Grand Bay   ▯▯▯▯

2669 S. Bayshore Drive
Coconut Grove, FL 33133
Tel. (305) 858-9600, fax 858-1532
Spacious luxury overlooking Biscayne Bay. Pool. 181 rooms.

Mayfair House   ▯▯▯/▯▯▯▯

3000 Florida Avenue
Coconut Grove, FL 33133
Tel. (305) 441-0000, fax 443-9284
All-suite hotel in the heart of the 'Grove'. Pool. 181 rooms.

Miami Airport Inn   ▯▯

1550 NW Lejeune Road
Miami, FL 33126
Tel. (305) 871-2345, fax 871-2811
Reasonable economy near international airport. Pool. 209 rooms.

Omni International   ▯▯▯

1601 Biscayne Boulevard
Miami, FL 33132
Tel. (305) 374-0000, fax 374-0020
Downtown 20-storey tower adjoining shopping mall. Pool. 550 rooms.

Sonesta Beach Key Biscayne   ▯▯▯▯

350 Ocean Drive
Key Biscayne, FL 33149
Tel. (305) 361-2021, fax 361-3096
Family-orientated resort on the ocean. Tennis, pools, golf course adjoining. 300 rooms.

THE GOLD COAST

Bahia Mar Resort   ▯▯/▯▯▯

801 Seabreeze Boulevard
Fort Lauderdale
Florida, FL 33316
Tel. (305) 764-2233, fax 524-6912
On the sea, with vast yacht and fishing marina adjoining. Tennis, pools, water sports. 300 rooms.

The Breakers   ▯▯▯/▯▯▯▯

1 S. County Road
Palm Beach, FL 33480
Tel. (407) 655-6611, fax 659-8403
Massive oceanfront palace dating from the 1920s, dominates the middle of Palm Beach. Two golf courses, tennis, croquet, pools. 528 rooms.

Days Inn   ▯/▯▯

1700 W. Broward Boulevard
Fort Lauderdale
Florida, FL 33312
Tel. (305) 463-2500, fax 763-6504
Economy in downtown Fort Lauderdale. Pool. 144 rooms.

Marriott Harbor Beach Resort   ▯▯▯/▯▯▯▯

3030 Holiday Drive
Fort Lauderdale, FL 33316
Tel. (305) 525-4000, fax 766-6165
Resort on Atlantic Ocean. Pools, tennis, water sports. 625 rooms.

Ocean Grand ▯▯▯/▯▯▯▯

2800 S. Ocean Boulevard
Palm Beach, FL 33480
Tel. (407) 582-2800, fax 547-1557

Newer luxury resort of low-rise buildings near the sea. Pools and gardens. 213 rooms.

Sheldon Ocean Resort ▯/▯▯

1000 N. Surf Road
Hollywood, FL 33019
Tel. (305) 922-6020, fax 922-6218

Budget hotel on ocean beach. 42 rooms.

Sheraton Bonaventure ▯▯▯/▯▯▯▯

250 Racquet Club Road
Fort Lauderdale
Florida, FL 33326
Tel. (305) 389-3300, fax 389-7810

Extensive resort some way inland. Golf, tennis, squash, health spa, pools. 500 rooms.

THE SPACE COAST AND ST AUGUSTINE

Anastasia Inn ▯▯

2050 Hwy A1A South
St Augustine Beach, FL 320
Tel. (904) 471-2575, fax 471-1247

Facing the Atlantic. Pool, water sports. 144 rooms.

Daytona Beach Hilton ▯▯/▯▯▯

2637 S. Atlantic Avenue
Daytona Beach, FL 32118
Tel. (904) 767-7350, fax 760-3651

On the ocean at the quieter end of the beach. Pool, tennis. 215 rooms.

Econo Lodge ▯

5500 N. Atlantic Avenue
Cocoa Beach, FL 32931
Tel. (407) 784-2550, fax 868-7124

Budget hotel near beach. Pool. 100 rooms.

Perry's Ocean Resort ▯▯

2209 S. Atlantic Avenue
Daytona Beach, FL 32118
Tel. (904) 255-0581, fax 258-7315

Beach-front hotel. Pools, water sports. 204 rooms.

Ponce de León Resort ▯▯▯

4000 US Hwy 1 North
St Augustine, FL 32085
Tel. (904) 824-2821, fax 829-6106

Country club setting. Golf, tennis, pools. Near beach. 230 rooms.

Wakulla Motel ▯▯

3550 N. Atlantic avenue
cocoa Beach, FL 32931
Tel. (407) 783-2230, fax 783-0980

Suite motel, each room with its own kitchen. Pools, gardens. Close to beach. 116 rooms.

69

WITHIN WALT DISNEY WORLD

Guests in Disney-owned accommodation have privileges in making reservations for shows, dinner, etc. Car parking at the theme parks is free for them, and entry to the parks by Disney transportation is guaranteed. These advantages can offset the somewhat higher prices of rooms within Disney World.

Caribbean Beach Resort   ▯▯

Walt Disney World
Lake Buena Vista, FL 32830
Tel. (407) 934-3400, fax 352-3202
Near EPCOT. Colourful 'village' design around a lake with themed pool and marina. 2112 rooms.

Contemporary Resort   ▯▯▯▯

Walt Disney World
Lake Buena Vista, FL 32830
Tel. (407) 824-1000, fax 352-3202
15-storey 'vaulting horse' shape, next to Magic Kingdom. Pools, marina. 1053 rooms.

Disney Inn   ▯▯▯

Walt Disney World
Lake Buena Vista, FL 32830
Tel. (407)824-2200, fax 352-3202
Near the Magic Kingdom, in quiet setting between two golf courses. Pools. 288 rooms.

Dixie Landings Resort   ▯▯

Walt Disney World
Lake Buena Vista, FL 32830
Tel. (407) 934-5800, fax 352-3202
Not far from EPCOT; convenient for all areas of WDW. Pools, waterway. 2048 rooms.

Grand Floridian Beach Resort   ▯▯▯▯

Walt Disney World
Lake Buena Vista, FL 32830
Tel. (407) 824-3000, fax 352-3202
Recreation of Victorian splendour. Monorail to Magic Kingdom. Pools, marina, beach. 901 rooms.

Walt Disney World Dolphin   ▯▯▯▯

Operated by Sheraton
PO Box 22653
Lake Buena Vista, FL 32830-2653
Tel. (407) 934-4000, fax 934-4880
Near EPCOT International Gateway. Vast triangular landmark tower. Marina, pools. 1509 rooms.

Walt Disney World Swan   ▯▯▯▯

Operated by Westin, PO Box 22786
Lake Buena Vista, FL 32830-2786
Tel. (407) 934-3000, fax 934-4499
A short walk to EPCOT International Gateway. Arc-roof tower topped by swans. Marina, pools, beach. 758 rooms.

Yacht Club & Beach Club Resorts ▐▐▐▐

Walt Disney World
Lake Buena Vista, FL 32830
Tel. (407) 934-7000 (Yacht Club),
934-8000 (Beach Club), fax 352-3202

Twin recreations of 19th-century Massachusetts coast resort. Marina, pools, beach. 1214 rooms.

DISNEY VILLAGE PLAZA

Designated 'Hotels of Walt Disney World', these are inside WDW but not Disney owned.

Buena Vista Palace ▐▐▐

1900 Buena Vista Drive
Lake Buena Vista, FL 32830
Tel. (407) 827-2727, fax 827-6034

Lakeside tower complex. Tennis, pools, gardens. 841 rooms.

Grosvenor Resort ▐▐▐

1850 Hotel Plaza Boulevard
Lake Buena Vista, FL 32830
Tel. (407) 828-4444, fax 828-8120

Tower block with convention facilities. Tennis, pools. 630 rooms.

Hilton ▐▐▐

1751 Hotel Plaza Boulevard
Lake Buena Vista, FL 32830
Tel. (407) 827-4000, fax 827-6380

C-shaped luxury block with restaurant, pools, tennis. 813 rooms.

Howard Johnson Resort Hotel ▐▐▐

1805 Hotel Plaza Boulevard
Lake Buena Vista, FL 32830
Tel. (407) 828-8888
fax 827-4623

14-storey tower and lower annexe. Pools, garden, family-orientated dining. 323 rooms.

ORLANDO AND AREA

Choice Inn ▐

4201 S. Orange Blossom Trail
Orlando, FL 32809
Tel. (407) 849-6110

Small economy hotel, south of downtown. Pool. 68 rooms.

Days Inn East of Magic Kingdom ▐▐

5820 W. Irlo Bronson
Memorial Hwy. (US192)
Kissimmee, FL 34746
Tel. (407) 396-1000
fax 396-1789

Budget hotel. Pools. 604 rooms.

Delta Orlando ▐▐

5715 Major Boulevard
Orlando, FL 32819
Tel. (407) 351-3340, fax 351-5117

Family-orientated budget resort. Pools, garden, tennis, mini-golf. 800 rooms.

Gateway Inn ▯▯

7050 Kirkman Road
Orlando, FL 32819
Tel. (407) 351-2000
fax 363-1835

Family-orientated economy hotel. Pools. 354 rooms.

Harley of Orlando ▯▯/▯▯▯

151 E. Washington Street
Orlando, FL 32801
Tel. (407) 841-3220
fax 841-3220 ext. 153

Downtown lakeside hotel. Near Church Street entertainment. Pool. 305 rooms.

Holiday Inn Winter Park ▯▯

626 Lee Road, Winter Park
Florida FL 32810
Tel. (407) 645-5600
fax 740-7912

Four miles north of downtown Orlando. Pools. 202 rooms.

Hyatt Regency Grand Cypress Resort ▯▯▯/▯▯▯▯

1 Grand Cypress Boulevard
Orlando, FL 32819
Tel. (407) 239-1234, fax 396-5090

Spacious resort and convention centre with golf courses, tennis, pools, lake, sailing, equestrian centre, large gardens. 750 rooms.

Larson's Lodge Maingate ▯

6075 W. Irlo Bronson
Memorial Hwy. (US192)
Kissimmee, FL 34746
Tel. (407) 396-6100, fax 396-6965

Budget hotel. Pools. 128 rooms.

Peabody Orlando ▯▯▯▯

9801 International Drive
Orlando, FL 32819
Tel. (407) 352-4000, fax 351-0073

Towering 27-storey landmark with convention centre. Tennis, pool. 851 rooms.

Stouffer Orlando Resort ▯▯▯

6677 Sea Harbor Drive
Orlando, FL 32821
Tel. (407) 351-5555, fax 351-9994

10-storey tower and convention complex, suited to families too. Pools, tennis. Close to Sea World. 778 rooms.

THE EVERGLADES

Flamingo Lodge ▯▯

PO Box 428, Flamingo
Everglades National Park
Florida, FL 33030
Tel. (305) 253-2241, (813) 695-3921

Base for sailing, fishing, exploring the national park. 120 rooms.

THE FLORIDA KEYS

Cheeca Lodge   ▦/▦▦

MM82, Overseas Hwy
Islamorada, FL 33036
Tel. (305) 664-4651, fax 664-2893
Luxury resort on the sea. Tennis, golf, pools, water sports. 203 rooms.

Pier House   ▦

1 Duval Street, Key West, FL 33040
Tel. (305) 296-4600, fax 296-7569
Next to Mallory Square and marina. Pool, small beach. 142 rooms.

La Terrazza de Marti ('La Te Da')   ▦/▦

1125 Duval Street
Key West, FL 33040
Tel. (305) 296-1075
Restored old house, now a 'boutique hotel' and fashionable magnet. Pool, entertainment. 18 rooms.

GULF COAST – NAPLES TO FORT MYERS

Days Inn Fort Myers Beach   ▦

8701 Estero Boulevard
Fort Myers Beach, FL 33931
Tel. and fax (813) 765-4422
Economy suite hotel with kitchen facilities. Pool, beach. 75 rooms.

Edgewater Beach   ▦/▦▦

1901 Gulfshore Boulevard North
Naples, FL 33940
Tel. (813) 262-6511, fax 262-1243
Quiet elegance facing directly on the beach. Pool. 124 rooms.

Lehigh Resort   ▦/▦

225 E. Joel Boulevard
Lehigh, FL 33936
Tel. (813) 369-2131
fax 369-2121 ext. 2291
Hotel situated in country club east of Fort Myers near I-75. Two 18-hole golf courses, floodlit tennis courts, pool. 121 rooms.

Park Shore Resort   ▦/▦

600 Neapolitan Way
Naples, FL 33940
Tel. (813) 263-2222
fax 263-0946
All-suite complex of villas with full kitchen facilities. Pool, landscaped gardens. 156 rooms.

Registry Resort   ▦/▦▦

475 Seagate Drive
Naples, FL 33940
Tel. (813) 597-3232
fax 597-3147
Spacious and elegant resort with golf, tennis, fitness facilities, pools, beach. 474 rooms.

Sundial Beach & Tennis Resort ▯▯▯

1451 Middle Gulf Drive
Sanibel Island
Florida, FL 33957
Tel. (813) 472 4151, fax 472-0554

Low-rise seafront resort with tennis courts and pools. 250 rooms.

Vanderbilt Inn ▯▯/▯▯▯

11000 Gulf Shore Drive North
Naples, FL 33963
Tel. (813) 597-3131
fax 597-3099

Smaller seafront resort north of Naples. Pools. 148 rooms.

GULF COAST – TAMPA BAY AREA

Best Western Safari ▯

4139 E. Busch Boulevard
Tampa, FL 33617
Tel. (813) 988-9191, fax 988-9195

Economy hotel close to Busch Gardens. Pool. 100 rooms.

Econo Lodge Resort ▯▯

5311 Ocean Boulevard
Sarasota, FL 34242
Tel. (813) 349-3211, fax 349-7915

Budget resort on Siesta Key, close to 'world's whitest sand'. Beach, pool. 50 rooms.

Holiday Inn Madeira Beach ▯▯

15208 Gulf Boulevard
Madeira Beach
Florida, FL 33708
Tel. (813) 392-2275
fax 392-2275 ext. 7143

On the white sandy beach north of St Pete's. Pool, water sports, tennis. 147 rooms.

Hyatt Sarasota ▯▯▯

1000 Boulevard of the Arts,
Sarasota
Florida FL 34236
Tel. (813) 366-9000, fax 952-1987

Near downtown, bay and Van Wezel Hall. Pool, marina. 297 rooms.

Sheraton Grand ▯▯▯

4860 W. Kennedy Boulevard
Tampa, FL 33609
Tel. (813) 286-4400, fax 286-4053

Close to International airport and Westshore business district. Large rooms, pool. 352 rooms.

Sirata Beach Resort ▯▯/▯▯▯

5390 Gulf Boulevard
St Petersburg Beach
Florida, FL 33706
Tel. (813) 367-2771, fax 360-6799

Family-orientated resort facing the beach. Pools, sports. 155 rooms.

Recommended Restaurants

Everywhere you turn, there's somewhere to eat, almost all open seven days a week. Here we give a selection of full-service restaurants, buffet restaurants and food courts (multiple outlets sharing a table area). There is no space to list even a fraction of the vast number of restaurants and all-you-can-eat buffets well within our lowest price range. (See also the section on Eating Out in the main part of this guide, pp.109–114.)

Each entry is marked with a symbol indicating the price range, per person, for a dinner comprising starter or salad, main course and dessert. (Drinks, gratuities and 6% sales tax are not included.)

▌	up to $15
▌▌	$15–30
▌▌▌	$30 and over

MIAMI AND MIAMI BEACH

A Mano ▌▌▌
1440 Ocean Drive, Miami Beach
Tel. (305) 531-6266
In the heart of the Art Deco district. Latin and Pacific flavours influence the 'New World cuisine'.

Brasserie LeCoze ▌▌▌
2901 Florida Avenue, Coconut Grove. Tel. (305) 444-9697
Classic French brasserie design and imaginative French/Mediterranean cooking.

Café Abbracci ▌▌▌
318 Aragon Avenue, Coral Gables
Tel. (305) 441-0700
Northern Italian cuisine.

Islas Canarias ▌
285 NW 27th Avenue, Miami
Tel. (305) 649-0440
Popular traditional Cuban cooking in Little Havana area.

Joe's Stone Crab ▌▌
227 Biscayne Street, Miami Beach
Tel. (305) 673-0365
An institution since 1913, open from October to May.

Malaga

740 SW 8th Street, Miami
Tel. (305) 858-4224

Traditional Cuban and Spanish dishes on 'Calle Ocho'.

Los Ranchos

Bayside Marketplace, Miami
Tel. (305) 375-0666

Nicaraguan-style steakhouse.

Rascal House

17190 Collins Avenue, Miami Beach. Tel. (305) 947-4581

New York-style deli known for its big sandwiches.

Sakura

8225 SW 124th Street, Miami
Tel. (305) 238-8462

Sushi, tempura, teriyaki dishes. One of many Japanese restaurants all over Miami.

WPA

685 Washington Avenue, Miami Beach. Tel. (305) 534-1684

Relaxed bistro-style modern American cooking with Italian and Tex-Mex variations.

Yuca

177 Giralda Avenue, Coral Gables
Tel. (305) 444-4448

Upscale, advanced Cuban cuisine in an elegant setting.

THE GOLD COAST

Café Arugula

3110 N. Federal Hwy Lighthouse Point. Tel. (305) 785-7732

The best and brightest ingredients in New American-Mediterranean cuisine.

Ruth's Chris Steak House

661 US Highway 1, North Palm Beach. Tel. (407) 863-0660

Specializing in steaks as well as seafood.

Studio One

2447 E. Sunrise Boulevard, Fort Lauderdale. Tel. (305) 565-2052

French and Caribbean-influenced cuisine.

Testa's

221 Royal Poinciana Way, Palm Beach. Tel. (407) 832-0992

Old established Italian and seafood eating place in garden courtyard.

TooJay's Gourmet Deli

313 Poinciana Place, Royal Poinciana Center, Palm Beach Tel. (407) 659-7232

Generous sandwiches and delicatessen favourites in a relaxed atmosphere.

THE SPACE COAST AND ST AUGUSTINE

Capt. Jack's on the Ocean

2929 South A1A, Beverly Beach Tel. (904) 439-1000
Bar-restaurant with fresh seafood and steaks, south of St Augustine.

Live Oak Inn

448 South Beach Street, Daytona Beach. Tel. (904) 252-4667
American menu in an elegant old house overlooking marina. Closed Mondays.

The Pier Restaurant

Cocoa Beach Pier 401 Meade Avenue, Cocoa Beach Tel. (407) 783-7549
Elegant dining on the old wooden pier.

Raintree

102 San Marco Avenue St Augustine. Tel. (904) 824-7211
International cuisine in elegant surroundings.

St Regis

509 Seabreeze Boulevard, Daytona Beach. Tel. (904) 252-8743
An old home converted to a bed-and-breakfast inn and restaurant. American home cooking.

WALT DISNEY WORLD (INCLUDING VILLAGE/PLAZA)

Akershus Restaurant

Norway Pavilion, EPCOT (Reservations at EPCOT Earth Station)
Norwegian buffet of hot and cold dishes, from herring and salmon to goats' cheese and desserts.

Biergarten Restaurant

Germany Pavilion, EPCOT (Reservations at EPCOT Earth Station)
Veal, smoked pork, bratwurst and other German specialities.

Bistro de Paris

France Pavilion, EPCOT (Reservations at EPCOT Earth Station)
Traditional French ambience. Colourful and inventive cuisine, the menu devised by master chefs.

Cape May café

Beach Club Resort Tel. (407) 934-3358
New England-style clambake every night. Seafood buffets.

Cap'n Jack's Oyster Bar

Disney Village Marketplace Tel (407) 828-3900
Crab, lobster, clams and oysters, plus vegetarian and non-seafood alternatives.

77

Le Cellier　　　　‖
Canada Pavilion, EPCOT
(No reservations)
Cafeteria service of international
and Canadian dishes.

Fireworks Factory　　‖
Pleasure Island
Tel. (407) 934-8989
Barbecues, smoked chicken, veg-
etarian and low-calorie dishes.

Harry's Safari Bar
and Grill　　　　　‖
Dolphin (Sheraton)
Tel. (407) 934-4000 ext. 6155
Safari decor, grilled seafood and
steaks.

Marrakesh　　　　‖‖
*Morocco Pavilion, EPCOT (Reser-
vations at EPCOT Earth Station)*
Couscous, kebabs, tadjine and
other Moroccan specialities.

Palio　　　　　　‖‖
Swan (Westin). Tel. (407) 934-1281
Northern Italian specialities in an
elegant setting. Strolling musicians.

San Angel Inn　　‖‖
*Mexico Pavilion, EPCOT (Reser-
vations at EPCOT Earth Station)*
Mexican dishes beside the River
of Time ride.

78

ORLANDO AND AREA

Bonanza　　　　　‖
3615 West Highway 192
Kissimmee
Tel. (407) 932-4464
Lavish buffet with entrée order.

Capriccio　　　　‖‖
Peabody Hotel
9801 International Drive, Orlando
Tel. (407) 352-4000
Genuine Italian country cooking.

Charlie's Lobster House
　　　　　　　　　‖
Mercado Mall
8445 International Drive, Orlando
Tel. (407) 352-6929
Everything in shells or scales, any
way you like.

Hard Rock Café　　‖
Universal Studios Florida
5800 Kirkman Road, Orlando
Tel. (407) 351-7625
Burgers and sandwiches, fries and
shakes. Entry from street as well
as from Studios.

Jordan's Grove　　‖‖
1300 S. Maitland Avenue, Maitland
Tel. (407) 628-0020
Modern American cuisine in the
setting of a gracious old house.

Lili Marlene's   ‖

Church Street Station, Orlando
Tel. (407) 422-2434

Standard American menu in an elegant 1890s revival setting.

Ming Court   ‖‖

9188 International Drive, Orlando
Tel. (407) 351-9988

Regional Chinese cooking in an elaborate setting.

Siam Orchid   ‖

7575 Republic Drive, Orlando
Tel. (407) 351-3935

The taste of Thai.

Western Steer   ‖

6315 International Drive, Orlando
Tel. (407) 363-0677

All-you-can-eat buffet with steak or seafood.

THE FLORIDA KEYS

A & B Lobster House   ‖

700 Front street, Key West
Tel. (305) 294-2536

Oysters, clams, shrimp, barbecues and a view of the harbour.

Balamonte's   ‖

1223 White Street, Key West
Tel. (305) 296 2200

Italian and seafood restaurant.

Half Shell Raw Bar   ‖

Lands End Village, Key West
Tel. (305) 294-7496

Café-bar by the marina. Oysters, clams, crabs and conch fritters.

Louie's Backyard   ‖‖

700 Waddell Avenue, Key West
Tel. (305) 294-1061

American cuisine by the sea.

Quay Restaurant   ‖

MM102.5, Key Largo
Tel. (305) 451-0943

Seafood, steaks and pastas on the waterfront.

Ship's Pub Galley   ‖

MM61, Duck Key
Tel. (305) 743-7000

Steak and seafood by the dockside.

Whale Harbor Inn   ‖

MM84, Islamorada
Tel. (305) 664-4959

Seafood buffet by the marina.

GULF COAST – NAPLES TO FORT MYERS

Chef's Garden   ‖‖

1300 3rd Street S., Naples
Tel. (305) 262-5500

Elegant restaurant serving international and original cuisine.

79

Farino's/Gilda's Casa Italiana ▦

4000 Tamiami Trail N., Naples
Tel. (813) 262-2883
Seafood, pastas and grills in an informal setting.

The Mucky Duck ▦

5500 Estero Boulevard, Fort Myers Beach. Tel. (813) 463-5519
Informal setting for grilled, steamed and deep-fried seafood.

Tootie McGregor's ▦

Fort Myers Country Club
McGregor Boulevard, Fort Myers
Tel. (813) 939-7300
Elegant club setting. Comprehensive menu; strong on seafood.

GULF COAST – TAMPA BAY AREA

L'Auberge du Bon Vivant ▦▦▦

7003 Gulf of Mexico Drive
Longboat Key, Sarasota
Tel. (813) 383-2421
Classic French and international dishes in a country inn setting.

Boathouse ▦

Hyatt Sarasota, 1000 Boulevard of the Arts, Sarasota
Tel. (813) 366-9000
Seafood, salads and sandwiches in an informal setting over the water.

Charlie's Crab ▦

St Armand's Circle, Sarasota
Tel. (813) 388-3964

Choice of seafood and home-made pasta, with meat and vegetarian alternatives.

Eugen's ▦

100 N. Indian Rocks Road
Belleair Bluffs.
Tel. (813) 585-6399

Seafood, lamb, German and Hungarian dishes.

Michael's on East ▦▦▦

1212 S. East Avenue
Midtown Plaza, Sarasota
Tel. (813) 366-0077

Lively menu of salads, pastas, meats and fish.

Pippindales ▦

Clearwater Beach Hilton, 715 S Gulf Boulevard, Clearwater Beach
Tel. (813) 447-9566

Excellent value American buffets.

Summerhouse ▦

6101 Midnight Pass Road, Siesta Key, Sarasota.
Tel. (813) 349-1100

Woodland setting for fish, lobster, crab, steaks and chicken.

The Florida Keys

Curving westward from below Miami, a 120-mile (190-km) chain of islands called the Keys is stitched together by 43 bridges and the world's longest ocean-going road. First built as the last stage of Flagler's East Coast Railroad, the **Overseas Highway** soars and leapfrogs out to the old naval town of Key West.

South from Homestead follow Highway 1, or take the quieter Card Sound Road, through 30 miles (50 km) of flat swampland where herons and storks have built their great untidy nests of sticks on the telephone poles. You'll soon be on **Key Largo**, largest of the islands. The southern end is a ribbon of the uglier sort of commercial development, but it's the base for trips to the **John Pennekamp State Park**, 27 miles (43 km) of coral reefs, tropical fish, sponges and ship-wrecks. Plenty of small shops rent diving equipment, cameras and boats. To scuba dive you need to be qualified: there are schools here where you can sign up for tuition. Glass-bottomed boats make regular trips along the reef for those who prefer to keep dry while admiring the fish. (Take an anti-seasickness pill if it's rough and you are susceptible.)

Moored at Mile Marker 100 (locations on the Keys are expressed in distances from Key West), the little steamboat *African Queen* was built in England in 1912 and used on Lake Albert in East Africa. She appears in the 1951 film star-ring Humphrey Bogart and Katherine Hepburn. Strictly speaking, though, she has no business to be here – Bogart didn't even make *Key Largo* on Key Largo.

Further down the Keys on the group of islands called **Islamorada**, you'll find plenty of opportunities for diving and snorkelling, as well as fishing for some of the estimated 600 species of fish. At one of the oldest marine shows in Florida, **Theater of the Sea**, cheerful young trainers lead visitors from one pool to another, pointing out dolphins, rays, sharks and sea lions. **81**

BUILDING BRIDGES

At many places along the way you'll see where the old Flagler railway viaducts were converted into a roadway after a hurricane destroyed several sections in 1935. Some abandoned sections of bridge make superb fishing piers, if you can keep the pelican competition at bay. The two-mile (3-km) **Long Key Viaduct** is one of the most striking achievements of the railway builders, and Long Key itself has a state park and campground.

Marathon, chief town of the Middle Keys, is a sizeable resort and a diving and fishing centre. The museum is informative on the geology of the Keys and their early inhabitants. After Marathon, Flagler's engineers met their biggest challenge, seven miles (11 km) of sea to be bridged on the way to the Lower Keys. The **Seven-Mile Bridge** still stands, a monument to the hundreds of workers who died between 1905 and 1912, the time it took to build the Overseas Railroad. Now it's

Don't Touch

A coral reef is alive and growing, the creation of billions of tiny polyps. Related to jellyfish and sea anemones, these little animals live in cup-shaped shells of limestone that they build for themselves. Coral's gorgeous colours come from algae living within the coral tissue. Each new generation builds on the skeletons of the last, but the outer living layer is thin and very fragile. A boat's anchor can leave a dead white scar. Even the touch of a diver's hand or foot can spread decay. In shallower water, corals resemble boulders and delicate fans. Further out, where they have to stand up to a battering from waves, come the branching elkhorn varieties. Even from a glass-bottom boat you'll see hosts of fish enjoying the reef's protection. Their bright colours probably relate to the need to distinguish foes from possible mates in the crowd.

defunct, replaced by a new road bridge with parapets frustratingly blocking the view. Stop at either end to see the bridges sweep over turquoise water into the misty distance.

Bahia Honda, a state recreation area and nature reserve, has a tropical sandy beach, something of a rarity in the Keys. You'll notice the strange double-decker bridge here: the road used to be on top.

At last the 2000-mile-long (3200 km) Highway 1 can go no further; you've reached the remote town of Key West, which has become as fashionable as Carmel in California or Provincetown on Cape Cod.

KEY WEST

The word 'Key' comes from the Spanish *cayo* meaning a small island. It is possible that Key West was named *Cayo Oesto* by Ponce de León. But for many years it was called *Cayo Hueso*, Bone Island, perhaps because Indian battles in the 18th century left the island littered with them. Pirates and wreckers were then the main

inhabitants until the US Navy came to plant the flag in 1822. But for all its violent past, Key West is one of the friendliest towns in Florida.

Four hours drive from Miami, the 1-by-3½-mile (1.6-by-5.6-km) subtropical island is actually nearer to Havana. Its population comprises retired military people, Cuban exiles, health-food buffs, hayfever sufferers who find the pure air here a boon, black and white descendants of the original 'conchs' who came from the Bahamas, writers, painters and a large gay community. Now they all claim to be conchs (pronounced 'konks'), after the big pink molluscs which cling to the underwater rocks.

You approach the island via the newer, commercial quarter. Follow the road to the old town, past an odd collection of hotels and motels, often with heated pools under tropical palms. (In season, you'll find Key West accommodation some of the most expensive in the United States.) In **Duval Street**, lined with shops selling arts and crafts, souvenirs, T-shirts and **83**

Key West, the rainbow's end.

trash, **Sloppy Joe's** is one of the noisiest of several bars. (The place which used to have that name – Ernest Hemingway's old haunt – is round the corner in Greene Street.)

Duval Street ends at **Old Mallory Square**, scene of a nightly free show. Towards sunset, a crowd gathers on this stone quay to be entertained by musicians, jugglers, fire-eaters and eccentrics.

Close by Mallory Square stands the terminal of the Conch Tour Train, a mock railway engine pulling rubber-wheeled buggies on a 14-mile (23-km) trip past the island's

sights. The Old Town Trolley company competes with it, and trishaws carry sightseers on shorter trips.

The **Ernest Hemingway House** (907 Whitehead Street), set in a tropical garden, was owned by the author for 30 years, although he lived here on and off for only about ten of them. But some of his most famous books, including *For Whom the Bell Tolls* and *A Farewell to Arms*, were at least partly written in Key West. A climb up the lighthouse opposite is worth it for the view.

The famous painter and naturalist, John James Audubon, came to Key West in 1832 to paint the birds of the Florida Keys. The so-called **Audubon House** has some good English furniture but only a tenuous connection with the man himself. It's a bit disillusioning to learn that the great naturalist was as fond of shooting birds as he was of painting them.

On Front Street, the **Mel Fisher Museum** displays finds from the *Nuestra Señora de Atocha*, one of eight Spanish galleons wrecked in a hurricane off this coast in 1622. After years of searching, Fisher found the treasure, valued at hundreds of millions of dollars, in 1985.

Stroll through the Truman Annex, an attractive redevelopment of former naval housing, to see the immaculately restored **Truman Little White House**, favourite retreat of President Harry S. Truman in the forties and fifties. Nearby in a small state park, there's not much left of Fort Zachary Taylor, but the beach is one of the best in the area. The intense sunshine here can be a problem, so take precautions against overexposure even walking the city streets. Fortunately, Smathers Beach towards the airport has the odd palm tree or two for shade. The **coral reef** offshore breaks the waves, creating a haven for snorkellers.

The Gulf Coast

Until recently, the Gulf Coast was a well-kept secret, one which European vacationers have only just begun to discover. The warm, calm waters and gently-sloping white sands are perfect for children, and there are plenty of **85** diversions away from the beaches. The rapidly developing towns from Naples to St Petersburg gleam in the sun, and business parks, shopping centres and residential developments are spreading inland. Old fishing towns are being gradually eclipsed by new construction.

Much of the coastline is protected by long offshore sandbars, which means crossing salt lagoons, by causeway or boat, to find the beach. From Marco Island near the Everglades up to Tampa Bay, 180 miles (290 km) of inlets, lakes, peninsulas and islands make for a sailing and fishing paradise.

Quiet seclusion on one of the many islands off the west coast of Central Florida.

The elegant town of **Naples** has a fishing pier and a famous shell beach, with collectors out early in the morning to see what the tide has left behind. The Village on Venetian Bay shows how attractive a shopping mall can be, and for a view of the most luxurious waterfront homes, take a dinner cruise on a stern-wheeler around the maze of inlets.

The **Teddy Bear Museum** (2511 Pine Ridge Road) is more like a vast shop, with a few historic and precious collector's items. Classic car fans will find the finest collection of Porsches outside the Stuttgart factory at **Collier Automotive Museum** (2500 S. Horseshoe Drive), along with historic racing cars. At the junction of Fleischmann Boulevard and US 41, **Jungle Larry's Zoological Park** features big-game animals and wild birds in a tropical garden.

If you'd prefer to see creatures in the wild, follow county road 846 to **Corkscrew Swamp**. The National Audubon Society has preserved a sanctuary of 11,000 acres (4400 ha) of wilderness here. Almost two miles (3 km) of boardwalks pass through the great bald cypress trees (so-called because they drop their needles in winter).

FORT MYERS

Just south of downtown Fort Myers you can visit the **Edison Winter Home** (2350 McGregor Boulevard). The inventive genius who gave the world the light bulb, the phonograph, the stock ticker and much more, Thomas Alva Edison (1847–1931) moved here for his health in 1886. He built a laboratory and developed the garden of exotic plants and trees in his search for new materials. The huge banyan tree was once a seedling, a gift from Harvey Firestone, founder of the tyre company. The tour takes in Edison's laboratory, a collection of old cars and phonographs and his **87**

study filled with personal effects. The great inventor's friend Henry Ford built a house right next door – you can visit that too, though it's not of such compelling interest.

Four miles (6.4 km) north of Fort Myers, the **Shell Factory** has a vast collection, but it's primarily a gift shop. In the same area you can tour a citrus packing and juice extraction plant, or head inland for an interesting visit to the **ECHO project**, off Durrance Road north-east of Fort Myers. Here in a programme to help combat world hunger, plants are tested under all sorts of conditions and the seeds of successful varieties are sent off to third world countries.

In the same area, the **Babcock Wilderness Adventure** (off State Road 31) takes you on a ride through swamp and forest, with stops to look at the wildlife. Alligators lying across the historic trails will make you appreciate the conditions the early pioneers had to contend with. You need to telephone for reservations; the number to call **88** is (813) 489-3911.

OFFSHORE RETREATS

Only specks on the Florida map, the string of islands that stretches like a fishhook from the mouth of the Caloosahatchee River across Charlotte Harbour are beloved and fiercely protected by their residents. **Sanibel**, the southernmost, is famous for its seashells and for the J.N. Darling National Wildlife Refuge. It's also well known for its traffic jams in high season, although you can't see much from a car and there are few places to stop. To appreciate this area and its wildlife you really need to take to the water. Tiny **Captiva** island is linked to Sanibel by a causeway but so far, North Captiva and Cayo Costa can only be reached by boat. **Boca Grande** (accessible by toll bridge via Englewood) has long been a winter hideaway for rich northerners.

North again on the mainland, **Venice** has some fine public beaches. It is also the winter headquarters of the Ringling Brothers Barnum and Bailey **Circus World**, since they relocated from Sarasota.

SARASOTA

This self-styled cultural capital of Florida is a favourite with visitors. The locals insist it's queen of the coast, with its own orchestra and winter seasons of ballet, opera and theatre.

Near the centre, the **Van Wezel Performing Arts Hall** is a landmark. Completed in 1970 and dubbed the 'purple people-seater', it rises by the Bay like a dramatic lavender shell. Downtown on Main Street, look for the biggest publishers' remainders bookshop outside New York City.

Sarasota's **Jungle Garden** is another of Florida's beautiful botanical gardens, stocked with a few jungle animals, and the **Selby Gardens** on the bay front have thousands of orchids and water lilies shaded by banyan trees and bamboo.

Across Ringling causeway off US 41, Sarasota's prettiest shopping and restaurant centre, **St Armand's Circle**, is on the way to Lido Key and Beach. The next barrier island to the south, **Siesta Key** claims the whitest sand in the world and

has the scientific data to prove it. Suitably wetted, it's superb for castle-building too. Low tide brings out the shell seekers, stooping and scraping.

John and Mable Ringling of circus fame established their **estate** just north of Sarasota in the early 1920s. Within just a few years the couple had built a Venetian-style palazzo and a museum filled with hundreds of works of art that reflected their passion for the Italian Renaissance and Baroque.

The **Ringling Museum** has several of the Rubens cartoons for the *Triumph of the Eucharist* cycle (the other two extant are in the Louvre in Paris). Hals, Cranach and Veronese are also represented in this superbly arranged collection of 14th- to 19th-century paintings. Don't miss the less-publicized paintings by Joseph Wright of Derby, Rosa Bonheur and Burne-Jones (the extraordinary *The Sirens*). Near the museum is the **Asolo Theater**, a Rococo gem brought stone by stone from Asolo, north-west of Venice, Italy, and reassembled here in the early 1950s.

89

A replica of Michelango's statue of David in the courtyard of the Ringling Museum.

Ca' d'Zan ('John's House' in Venetian patois) has been called grandiose but if the Ringlings wanted a house in Venetian palace style, why not? It's undeniably impressive, on the shores of the bay. The crystal chandelier came from New York's Waldorf-Astoria Hotel, while the oak and stained glass bar was copied from one in St Louis, where John reportedly spent a good deal of time drinking with his buddies.

The Museum of the Circus in the grounds, with its gilt circus wagons and old posters, was an afterthought on the part of the State, to which Ringling left his estate and collections.

A huge range of old cars and 2000 mechanical musical instruments – player pianos, fairground organs, musical boxes and phonographs – can be seen at **Bellm's Cars and Music of Yesterday**, just across US 41.

East of Sarasota on Route 72, you can bike, drive or take a boat trip through the **Myakka River State Park** or hike along the 37 miles (60 km) of nature trails.

ST PETERSBURG

Continuing up the coast, the impressive Sunshine Skyway toll bridge soars high over the mouth of Tampa Bay. On the north side, St Petersburg is a quiet, sprawling city, where motel and restaurant prices are reasonable. Americans think of 'St Pete' as full of retired people, but in recent years a lot of businesses have moved here and the downtown area is in the throes of renewal. A strange-looking inverted pyramid apparently floating in the water is **Pier Place**, a complex of shops with a food court and a restaurant on top. The half-mile-long (0.8 km) pier is the starting point for fishing trips and pleasure cruises.

A few blocks away on 4th Street the **Sunken Gardens** are a tropical riot of colour, with wildlife and bird life amid the bougainvillea and, if you like, 'the world's largest gift shop'.

The **Salvador Dali Museum** (1000 3rd Street South) was donated to the city by two friends of Dali from Cleveland, Ohio. Opened in **91**

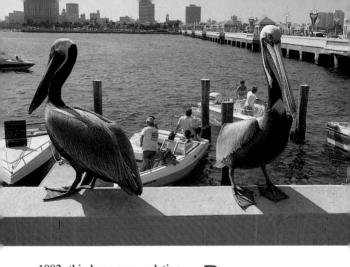

1982, this huge accumulation of works by the Spanish surrealist includes paintings, sculptures and graphics. If you find so much Dali a touch indigestible, there's an anti-dote waiting at the **Fine Arts Museum** on the street leading to the pier. Eclectic and accessible, with works by Renoir and Cézanne, and American painters Georgia O'Keeffe, Whistler and Grandma Moses, this collection is a delight.

PINELLAS SUNCOAST

St Petersburg faces the Bay, but several miles away on the Gulf

Pelicans are as common as pigeons on the Florida coast.

Coast **St Petersburg Beach** is the start of a 20-mile (32-km) string of barrier islands stretching north to **Clearwater Beach,** and sometimes known collectively as the Pinellas Suncoast. Reached by four causeways, the strip is built-up from end to end with hotels, motels, apartment blocks, fast-food outlets and restaurants. But don't be put off: the gently-sloping sandy beach is superb, up to two hundred yards (183 m) wide, with occasional piers for fishing. The sunsets are legendary, blending crimson and purple velvet.

At John's Pass, the sea separates Madeira and Treasure Island, and a bridge links them. The Village and Boardwalk here are a complex of restaurants, bars and shops. Clearwater Beach has some bigger hotels and condominiums and has jumped up in the European holiday charts.

North of Clearwater, **Tarpon Springs** became the home of the sponge industry when Greek divers were brought here at the beginning of the 20th century. Despite diseases and competition from synthetic sponges, it's still going, though shrimp-fishing is much more important now. At **Spongeorama** you can learn about the history of sponge-diving and visit various exhibits about the marine creature whose skeleton ends up in your bath.

Thirty miles (48 km) up the coast the **Weeki Wachee** theme park features birds-of-prey shows and water slides, but the main attraction is an improbable underwater ballet *The Little Mermaid*. Maidens with flowing hair and fishtails hold their breath, smile bravely and perform acrobatics.

TAMPA

The big city of the Gulf Coast is still quite compact, but growing fast, upwards in the centre and outwards away from the Bay. Major restoration is in progress at **Ybor City**, where there were once 200 cigar factories employing thousands of Cuban workers, displaced from their homeland in the 19th century. The depression of the 1930s dealt the industry a near-fatal blow.

The area along 7th and 8th Avenues between 13th and 22nd Streets has remained like a time warp. Now, among the Cuban snack bars and little businesses, souvenir shops, antique shops and fancier restaurants have sprung up. You can learn something of the history of Ybor City at the museum (1818 Ninth Avenue). **93**

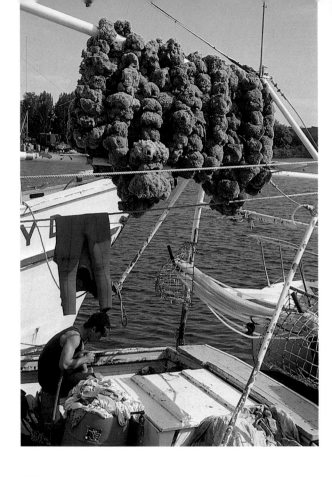

The sponge-diving industry of Tarpon Springs still survives to this day.

BUSCH GARDENS

In a huge 300-acre (120-ha) park north-east of Tampa, brewing giants Anheuser-Busch have piled on the attractions as if they were trying to outdo all their rivals. 'The Dark Continent' is the overall theme and the buildings are just like southern Morocco. Collect a map at the entrance: the layout is confusing.

The open plains of the **Serengeti** with their big game animals and herds of grazing zebras and antelopes can be viewed from cable cars, a monorail or an old-fashioned train. Try all three. You can go white-water rafting on the Congo River or scream down a waterfall. There's an ice show and a thrilling simulator ride, **Questor**, supposedly an eccentric British professor's universal travelling machine. The Python and Scorpion **roller coasters** turn you upside-down at breakneck speed, and a giant swingboat, **The Phoenix**, does the same thing very slowly.

You are invited to tour the on-site brewery and to sample the beers at Hospitality House if you are 21 years of age or over. You can easily take a full day to see Busch Gardens and get value for your money.

Nearby **Adventure Island** water park (same owners) has waterfalls, waterslides and waves. It closes in winter.

A family outing to Busch Gardens, north-east of Tampa.

What to Do

Sports

With a winter like other people's summers and seas as tempting as a tropical lagoon, Florida will have you out and playing before you can get your bags unpacked.

Golf and tennis practically have the status of religions here. The waters are ideal for sailing, canoeing and fishing. You can go hiking, riding and hunting (here it means shooting). Spectator sports at various times of year include football, baseball, basketball and even polo. You can watch and bet on greyhounds and horses and the local speciality, jai alai, a super-fast version of squash played with a hybrid of a hockey stick and a sling.

Sports cars, grand prix cars and stock cars race the famous tracks at Daytona and Sebring and the streets of Miami. Then there's the most popular outdoor activity of all – hitting the beach and occasionally cooling off in the sea.

WATER SPORTS

Practically everyone's first idea is to get on, into or under the water. Whether you prefer windsurfing, scuba diving, water-skiing or just plain swimming, Florida's beaches and sheltered inland waterways have room enough for everybody.

Chances for **scuba diving** exist along the Atlantic coast, but the best area is around the Florida Keys including more than 20 miles (32 km) of coral reef in John Pennekamp State Park (see p. 81). You'll need a certified diver's card or else to take classes when you arrive; details can be obtained from any diving shop.

Snorkelling amid the brilliant fish is exhilarating too. Everyone is urged not even to touch the coral, and it's illegal to take any of it. You can hire all the necessary equipment: shop around for the best prices.

Big waves for **surfing** are mainly restricted to the Atlantic coast – Cocoa Beach and Melbourne Beach are favourites. Waters protected by Florida's many barrier islands or the generally calmer seas of the Gulf Coast are ideal for **water-skiing** or **windsurfing**.

With a coastline this long, **beaches** are countless – and often almost endless (Daytona's, for instance, runs for 23 miles/37 km), though access may be restricted by private property. If the crowd is too dense for you in one spot, a short walk will earn you some solitude – most people don't stray far from their cars.

There's an occasional problem with jellyfish, including the stinging Portuguese man-of-war, or accumulations of weed, and Atlantic storms can sometimes wash away a stretch of sand.

Popular beaches usually have lifeguards, especially at weekends. Many have barbecue facilities too, but alcohol, glass containers and pets are frequently banned.

Beware of the power of the sun, especially if you are snorkelling: your back can feel cool and still burn quite badly, unless you've applied waterproof sunblock.

BOATING AND SAILING

No holiday in Florida would be complete without at least one outing on the water. Power-boats, sailboats and canoes in profusion are available for hire. You can sail nearly everywhere. Some of the best powerboating is from Everglades City among the Ten Thousand Islands and down south in Florida Bay. Navigational charts are available at marinas and map dealers.

Airboat rides are a noisy but exciting way of skimming shallows and swamps and **glass-bottom boats** let you see the coral reefs without getting wet.

There are also some 35 official **canoeing** trails through the Everglades and on the rivers flowing from central Florida's springs and lakes. The state's Department of Natural Resources publishes a free guide (3900 Commonwealth Boulevard, Tallahassee, FL 32399-3000). To hire canoes look in the Yellow Pages under Boat Dealers, or ask at the local chamber of commerce.

97

FISHING

Hundreds of different species of fish inhabit the rivers, creeks and seas. You can hire rods and reels, or if you're an enthusiast, this is a good place to buy equipment. Bait shops at the docks and fishing piers will give you free advice on what to fish for. Often your biggest problem will be competition from pelicans, who hang about in the hopes of stealing away with some of your catch. In the process they may get hooked themselves: if it happens, release them with extreme care. (Get help if you can.)

Marinas everywhere are crowded with expensive deep-sea fishing boats for hire – they come complete with a knowledgeable captain. Beyond that the only thing you'll need is plenty of patience. Some boats go for the more certain mackerel and amberjack, but you can try for the big ones – marlin and shark, or the exciting if inedible tarpon which can weigh from 60–100 lbs (30–45 kg).

A number of resorts have a branch of FISH (Florida Inland Sportsfishing Hosts), dedicated to making you a regular visitor to the local lakes and rivers. They publish brochures mapping the waters, listing accommodations, campgrounds and fishing regulations. Okeechobee is good for lake fishing and big bass are also found in the rivers or in Lake George. Canals are well-stocked and sometimes turn up saltwater fish such as tarpon or snook.

For more information on boating and fishing, write to the Department of Natural

Coconut Grove harbour. **99**

Resources, 3900 Commonwealth Boulevard, Tallahassee, FL 32399-3000. You'll need a visitor's licence if you are over 16 and plan to do any fishing, whether saltwater or freshwater. These are available at marinas and tackle shops.

HIKING

Most people stick to walking or jogging along the beaches but there are plenty of marked trails in the national forests and state parks.

Only members of the Florida Trail Association may use trails across private property. Membership isn't expensive. Write to: Florida Trail Association Inc, PO Box 13708, Gainesville, Florida, FL 32604.

GOLF

There are over 1,000 golf courses in the state of Florida – over 40 courses in Greater Miami alone, plus a heavy concentration up the Gold Coast, the Gulf Coast, the centre and the north of Florida. Some

holiday companies offer packages including green fees, but even the regular prices are reasonable, especially if you start after 3 p.m. If you haven't brought your equipment, clubs and even shoes are for rent at some courses, and Florida abounds with golf shops. You may be required to hire and use a ride-on buggy (and to heed warnings not to run over any alligators). Local Chambers of Commerce will supply lists of courses.

Resort courses have plenty of staff who need tipping: they won't let you carry your clubs at all. Avoid playing at midday in summer. Even the usually ubiquitous drinks carts can't make it pleasurable. Rates are lower in summer when the crowds have gone.

TENNIS

Many larger hotels have courts; some resorts have teaching facilities and organize tournaments. Miami Beach has nearly 50 courts in two separate tennis centres. In Orlando you can book the clay courts of Orlando

Tennis Club or the asphalt ones at the public club in Winter Park. Walt Disney World's Contemporary Resort has a tennis clinic with video equipment, practice lanes and automatic ball machines. Anywhere in Florida you won't be far from a tennis club, but in summer it's best to play in the early morning or late afternoon, avoiding the punishing combination of hot sun and humidity.

HUNTING

Most tourists on a two-week jaunt to Florida don't come for the hunting scene. Nevertheless, parts of northern Florida offer the best wild turkey shooting; rabbit, fox and raccoon can be shot almost everywhere, and deer in some wilder districts.

Licences are necessary. Contact the Game and Freshwater Fish Commission for further details.

Florida is a mecca for tennis players, both amateur and professional.

SPECTATOR SPORTS

The climate makes the state ideal for northern **baseball** teams to keep fit during the winter. The Boston Red Sox, Baltimore Orioles and many others play spring training games in several Florida cities.

In professional **football**, Miami has its famous Dolphins, who play at the Joe Robbie Stadium, and Tampa Bay is the base of the Buccaneers. Miami's huge **Orange Bowl** is home to the University of Miami Hurricanes and on 1 January each year the two top college teams meet in the Orange Bowl Classic.

Florida hosts some major **tennis** tournaments, notably the Lipton International on Key Biscayne in March.

As for professional **golf**, the Doral-Ryder PGA Open is held in Miami every February or March, followed by the Honda Classic.

Horse racing takes place at Miami's Hialeah Park (short winter season), Calder Race Course just north of Miami, Gulfstream Park at Hallandale,

Florida Downs at Tampa (January to mid-March) and Gator Down, Pompano which also has harness racing. (See the local press for details.) **Greyhound racing** venues include Daytona, Hollywood, Key West, Miami, Orlando and Tampa. If you prefer a more rarefied entertainment, **polo** is a popular winter sport at Boca Raton.

Most intriguing to a visitor is the action-packed Basque game of **jai alai** (pronounced 'high ligh'). You'll see it played at night in season at the Miami Fronton (3500 NW 37th Avenue), and at Dania, Daytona and Tampa. Tickets are cheap, because the idea is to get you in to bet on the *parimutuel* (tote) system, which also runs the gambling at the dog and horse races.

Finally, **cars** and **motorbikes** race at Daytona International Speedway. In February thousands gather for the famous Daytona 500, and the central

Colourful cloth weavings produced by local Seminole Indians.

Florida town of Sebring stages its 12-hour international sports car race every March. Miami's Grand Prix in Monaco-style uses city streets including Biscayne Boulevard.

Shopping

America's marketing wizards can come up with bargains in every sort of product, as well as a vast choice. Check the prices the discount stores advertise in weekend editions of the local newspapers. If you're attracted by electrical goods, don't forget that American equipment runs on 110 volts, so make sure that what you buy can be adapted to your home voltage, if necessary.

Prices vary enormously from store to store. A swimsuit bought at a sea-front hotel

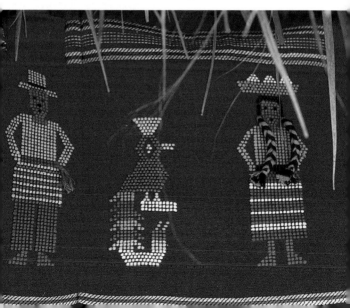

boutique may be four times the cost of an identical one in a department store 200 yards away. It pays to shop around.

Even better bargains are found at the sales which most stores hold several times a year, usually after Christmas, the 4th of July and other holidays. A sales tax of around 6% is added to the ticket price of all purchases.

WHEN AND WHERE TO SHOP

Hours vary: suburban malls are open 7 days a week, 10 a.m. to 9 p.m., while shops in city centres are generally open only until around 5.30 p.m., closing on Sundays. Large chain stores close only for national holidays – and not all of them.

In addition to the shopping centres, supermarkets, speciality shops, discount and chain stores, Florida has a style of shopping found only in the world's prosperous places: prestige malls. The very buildings reflect the wares within. Featuring tropical landscaping, modern sculpture and

fountains, they are often innovatively designed by creative architects. Inside, the best of American designer boutiques, antique and jewellery shops alternate with branches of famous European fashion houses. Even if the prices are out of your league, there's nothing to stop you from window shopping.

WHAT TO BUY

Florida keeps its eyes on Europe, New York and California, and responds to fashion with the latest in **leisurewear**, swimsuits, robes and shoes.

'Western stores' sell leather goods and **cowboy clothes**. This is a cattle state so they actually supply real cowboys and ranchers, not just tourists, though the merchandise these days is not always made in the United States. A well-fitting pair of cowboy boots will last for years. You can also get fringed Indian jackets, jeans, silver buckles, leather hats and gloves and tooled leather handbags and wallets.

Some stores stock **Indian crafts** from all over America,

including fine woven blankets, ponchos, wall hangings and skirts. The local Seminoles specialize in patchwork children's clothing. You can bargain for semi-precious jewellery, often turquoise stones set in silverwork, and artistic pottery. The prices may seem a bit high – they've risen considerably in recent years.

It might seem strange to come here and buy oriental goods but the import stores have bargains in woven raffia, wood, leather and wicker furniture and rugs.

America is the natural home of gadgets and electronic marvels, from toys to laptop computers – many of them imported, but often cheaper here. **Sports** players should check out the equipment on offer, especially for golf, tennis and fishing.

And finally, you can send back a box of Florida sunshine. The larger roadside stands will pack their own tangerines, oranges, grapefruits or a mixture and ship it home for you – if local laws permit. (See p. 114.)

Entertainment

In downtown **Miami** and concentrated in Little Havana, the dominant note is Cuban, the exiles showing what, for better or worse, the old country was like before the revolution. Supper-clubs and *discotecas* raise the temperature with the latest merengue, salsa and cumbia sounds. 'Anglos' may need to take some lessons before going public on the dance floor in a lambada. For them the choice widens in **Miami Beach**, especially along trendy Ocean Drive and Washington Avenue in South Beach where bars and restaurants feature live jazz and clubs come and go with bewildering speed. Rock, reggae, '60s revival and gay clubs, British and Irish pubs – any excuse for drinking and dancing will do.

The scene is just as varied in **Coconut Grove**. On Friday and Saturday nights you'll think everyone in Miami has come here to cruise the streets and pack the bars. Music blares from cars and cafés until the small hours, and street **105**

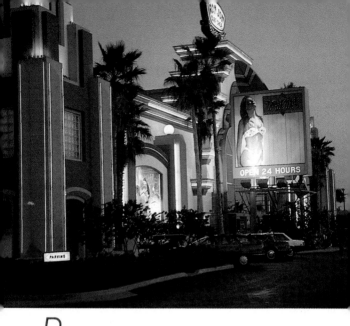

Buy your goggles and snorkels in the middle of the night at Ron Jon Surf Shop in Cocoa Beach.

performers entertain the crowd. If you prefer something quieter, Miami and the Beach also have dozens of piano-bars. Some agencies organize tours of the nightclubs in a package that includes cocktails at one and dinner at another, sometimes followed by a floor show.

Orlando has cashed in on the theme park traffic with nightclubs, western saloons and cancan dancers on the bar, in and around downtown Church Street Station. Walt Disney World tries to keep its guests on site for the evenings with all-American music – Dixieland, folk, Country and Western, disco and heavy metal – in the bars and dance halls of Pleasure Island. Disney's hotels have shows of their own, from Tahitian hula dancing at the Polynesian Resort to Broadway-type musical spectacles at the Contemporary Resort.

Other themed dinner-show packages in the Orlando area include 'Arabian Nights' (with 60 horses), 'Fort Liberty' (Wild West), 'King Henry's Feast' and 'Medieval Times'. You'll be elbow to elbow and the humour is unsubtle, but they're competitively priced, well-organized and fun.

THEATRE, CONCERTS, OPERA AND BALLET

Broadway sends touring shows to Miami Beach's Jackie Gleason Theater, the Coconut Grove Playhouse and to Palm Beach, Fort Lauderdale and Sarasota. That specially American institution, the dinner-theatre, where you can get a meal and a play, neither of them too heavy, is available at Fort Lauderdale and Tampa.

Both classical and rock concerts take place year-round in Miami at the Gusman Center for the Performing Arts and the Convention Center across from Du Pont Plaza. Dade Country Auditorium (2901 West Flagler Street) is the venue for the winter seasons of Greater Miami Opera and the world-class Miami City Ballet.

Sarasota declares itself to be the cultural capital of the state and backs up the claim with concerts, ballet, opera and theatre performances at the Van Wezel Hall and at the Ringling Museum's Asolo Center.

Key West specializes in casual live music in its bars and cafés. The Tennessee Williams Playhouse, as its name might suggest, offers drama a little more demanding than the musical comedies up the coast.

To find out about events in other Florida cities and towns, check the weekend newspapers. Many more than we can mention here have their own theatres and cinemas, and you're always within reach of a disco, club or bar with some sort of entertainment. **107**

Calendar of Events

Few states can match the sheer number of special events held annually in Florida. A few are listed here: buy a copy of the *What's On* magazine for more details.

January

> *Greek Festival* (Tarpon Springs). The Greek community of this west coast town celebrates its heritage.
>
> *Art Deco Weekend* (Miami Beach).
>
> *Three Kings Parade* (Miami's Little Havana). Latin spectacle, with bands, floats, marching and dancing.

February

> *Silver Spurs Rodeo* (Kissimmee). A semi-annual fair with calf-roping, steer-wrestling and other cowboy feats.
>
> *Old Island Days* (Key West). Conch-blowing contest, parades and other events commemorate the early history of the island.
>
> *Big Orange Music Festival* (Miami). Dade county-wide celebration, featuring every type of music from classical to rock.

March/April

> *Easter Sunrise Service* (Cypress Gardens). A service held at dawn on Easter Sunday.

April

> *Miami Grand Prix.*

July

> *4th July, Independence Day.* Special events everywhere. Bayside extravaganza in Miami.
>
> *Silver Spurs Rodeo* (Kissimmee). February event repeated.
>
> *All-American Water-Ski Championship* (Cypress Gardens). The pros contend in Florida's water-skiing capital.

September

> *Anniversary of the Founding of St Augustine* (St Augustine).

October

> *Hispanic Heritage Week Gala* (Miami). Art exhibits, lectures and other events.

December/January

> *Orange Bowl Festival* (Miami). Highlight is the Orange Bowl Parade on New Year's Eve.

Eating Out

Newcomers gasp at the prodigality of it all. So much to eat, so many places to choose from. You'll think half the population eats out all the time, and the other half run the massive food service. It's not so far from the truth.

Florida is a veritable cornucopia of citrus fruit, vegetables, salad crops, beef, fish and shellfish. Anything missing is simply shipped in.

WHEN TO EAT

Florida restaurants keep fairly flexible hours, and you'll find some places are even open round the clock. Breakfast is served from 6 or 7 to 11 a.m., lunch from about 11.30 a.m. to 1.30 p.m. and dinner from 5 or 6 until 9 or 10 p.m. Brunch is featured on Sundays between 11 a.m. and 3 p.m. Some restaurants offer an 'early-bird special', dinner at a lower price if you order before 5 or 6 p.m.

Spoilt for Choice

Your eating options are as varied as the strands that make up the population - and then some. Italian, Spanish, Mexican, Chinese, Thai, Vietnamese, Japanese, Greek, French – even British pubs serving fish and chips. Cuban cooking prevails in much of Miami, with Haitian and other Caribbean cuisines making an impact, and the Jewish community has brought the best of delicatessen food from New York.

Home-grown styles include the old stand-by of steak, salad and a baked potato, Cajun from Louisiana and 'new-American', taking ideas from all over but especially the Pacific rim. And remember, this is part of the South so you'll be offered grits (like unsweetened semolina) and gumbo (spicy stew with okra). In northern Florida you'll see hog jowls and collard greens in the supermarkets and boiled peanuts on the roadside stalls – a gastronomic trip for the adventurous!

WHERE TO EAT

Fierce competition has resulted in amazing bargains and reasonable quality at the lower end of the price range – fast-food, ethnic and 'family' restaurants and the all-you-can-eat buffets are usually very good value. A more elegant meal will cost from twice to ten times as much – sometimes worth the extra expense. Seek local advice if you can – hotel staff are often experts and free with their opinions. (See also HOTELS AND RESTAURANTS section.)

You can dine indoors in air-conditioned comfort or (more rarely) outside with a view of the sea or tropical gardens. Wherever you go, the emphasis is on informality.

Delicatessen restaurants specialize in gargantuan sandwiches of corned beef, smoked turkey, roast beef, and many other fillings. Cream cheese and lox (smoked salmon) on a bagel (a kind of firm bread roll) ranks high among kosher specialities, along with chopped liver and pastrami.

Takeaways. As well as the fast-food outlets, the delicatessen or cold meat counters in the better supermarkets are a

*G*ourmet cuisine in a greenhouse atmosphere.

great place to pick up a **picnic**. Just buy bread, order slices of whatever takes your fancy, add some fresh fruit and healthy salads (they come in handy containers and plastic cutlery is often supplied) and you're all set.

Breakfast. Continental breakfast comprises orange or grapefruit juice (it should be fresh), coffee and toast or a sweet pastry. Eggs appear on every menu, along with bacon, grits and sausages, French toast, waffles, pancakes and bagels.

European visitors may find American coffee rather weak, although refills are offered as a matter of course. If you crave more flavour, find a Cuban snack bar or coffee stall and drink little cups of aromatic *café cubano*. *Buche* is the strong black espresso variety.

Soups. You can almost make a meal of thick and filling seafood bisque, navy bean or Cuban black bean soup. Conch chowder, available on the Keys, combines milk, potatoes, vegetables, spices and chopped conch, a type of shellfish.

Salads. Many restaurants offer self-service salad bars with colourful displays of lettuce, raw vegetables, bean sprouts, olives, tomatoes, cottage cheese and fruits. Otherwise, a salad frequently 'comes with' the main course you select, though it's served before. Chef's salad is a meal in itself made with lettuce, cheese, ham, turkey or other cold meats.

Seafood. Florida's abundant fish and shellfish include red snapper, yellowtail, grouper, jumbo shrimp, stone crab and crawfish ('Florida lobster'). Don't be afraid to order dolphin, not the friendly mammal but a tasty fish. A lot of restaurants avoid confusion by using the Hawaiian name *mahi mahi*.

Nothing compares with the flavour of freshly caught broiled (grilled) fish, served with a simple lemon and butter sauce. In the cheapest places **111** it's unlikely to be fresh from the sea, but will probably have been frozen. There's a tendency to 'bread' everything, so specify if you don't want that. Shrimps come broiled, fried or steamed – sometimes in beer.

Stone crabs, a seasonal delicacy, have a devoted following all over southern Florida. Diners don bibs to eat the meat, extracting it from the claws with the aid of a nutcracker and dipping it into a lemon and butter or mustard and mayonnaise sauce.

You'll often see 'Raw Bars' advertised. These places usually serve oysters – often the only raw seafood actually on offer.

If the names confuse you, order a combination seafood platter, a sampling of the catch, served hot or cold. Meat lovers can have their steak and eat seafood too – 'Surf and Turf' is a steak and seafood platter.

You may get a taste for conch fritters (deep-fried pieces of the shellfish), especially on the Keys. Chefs inland favour catfish, a freshwater variety that is fried and served with hush puppies (not shoes but fried cornmeal balls).

Meats. Steaks, roast beef and southern fried chicken dominate. Whether you order your steak rare, medium-rare, medium or well done, you can be sure they'll get it just right.

Most Cuban restaurants offer *picadillo* (marinated ground beef mixed with olives, green peppers, garlic, onions and tomato sauce) and *arroz con pollo* (chicken and rice). A popular Mexican dish is *enchilada*, a tortilla (cornmeal pancake) stuffed with a meat filling and baked with sauce. *Tacos* can be eaten with *guacamole*, an avocado paste, or stuffed with ground beef and beans.

Vegetables. Except at some health-food and ethnic restaurants, cooked vegetables are not served in great variety; salads generally take their place. A notable exception is fresh corn on the cob. Yams, candied and baked, are a legacy of the Old South and the starchy root yuca features on some Cuban menus.

Desserts. Fruit pies are a standard on many menus along with dozens of flavours of ice cream and different sundaes and parfaits (alternate layers of fruit or sauce and ice cream in a tall dessert glass). Frozen yoghurt in fruit flavours is a diet-conscious alternative.

Sweet and creamy Key lime pie turns up everywhere in Florida, but especially on the Keys. Boston cream pie is a sponge cake filled with custard and topped with rich chocolate. Cheesecake reigns supreme in half a dozen varieties (strawberry, blueberry, pineapple – and of course Key lime).

Drinks. Fresh fruit juices are excellent. The big brand-name soft drinks are everywhere; iced water is almost universal and iced tea is an American speciality.

Cold beer is comparable to European lager but standard US brands taste sweeter. The 'dry' variants may suit your palate better. If not, many foreign beers are either imported or manufactured under licence. 'Light' (or 'Lite') doesn't mean low alcohol here, just lower in calories, so watch out.

House wines come by the bottle, carafe, or glass. If you order from the list, the French and Italian wines are generally no better than the Californian at similar prices. Some restaurants have no licence to sell wine, but won't mind if you bring your own bottle. The waiter will open it and provide glasses for a small charge.

Cocktails are served by the glass or, more economically, by the pitcher. The ever-popular piña colada combines rum, pineapple juice and coconut milk. Daiquiris are made with rum and an assortment of fruit juices – peach, strawberry or banana, for example. Mimosa is champagne and orange juice and a margarita is a mixture of fresh lime juice, tequila and ice.

A warning: liquor laws are strictly enforced. You can buy beer and wine in many grocery stores, but spirits are sold only in liquor stores. Cans and bottles of beer, wine or spirits must not be displayed in public places, but be kept in bags at all times. Alcohol is prohibited on many beaches, and no one under 21 years of age is permitted to buy alcohol. You may be asked for 'ID', an identification document showing your date of birth.

Florida Gold

The state's vast citrus groves make it America's and the world's biggest producer of many varieties. Growers large and small have assortments packed ready to send off as soon as an order is received.

The variety is vast, and yet new types continue to be developed. Here are some of the most popular ones:

Navel oranges: Easy to peel, thin-skinned and juicy, navels are in season in November.

Temple oranges: Richer in flavour than navels, temples peel like a tangerine – and are virtually seedless. They ripen in January and February.

Valencia oranges: Late-ripeners, Valencias appear at the fruit stands from March to May. They're particularly tasty in fruit salads.

Tangerines: Robinson tangerines ripen in October and November. In December and January you'll find the Dancy variety; in March, the extra-sweet Honey tangerines.

Tangelos: A Florida hybrid, tangelos combine the easy-eating qualities of the tangerine with the flavour of a sweet grapefruit.

Grapefruit: From the Indian River district, Marsh Whites have a nobler, austere acidity; Ruby Reds are sweeter.

Pomelos: Like a bigger, coarser, sweeter grapefruit.

Kumquats: Farmers often give away these little treats, which look like miniature, oval oranges. You eat the whole thing, sweet rind and all. Ask for some when you buy fruit.

Limes: Put an aromatic slice of green lime in your gin and tonic and you'll never go back to lemon.

BLUEPRINT
for a Perfect Trip

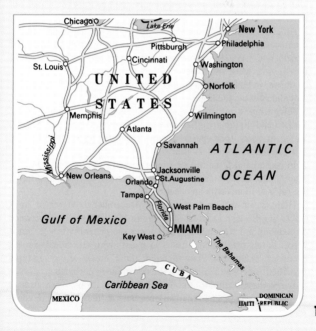

An A–Z Summary of Practical Information and Facts

A

ACCOMMODATION. See also HOTELS AND RESTAURANTS section, CAMPING and YOUTH HOSTELS.

Florida offers a huge variety of accommodation in every price range. However, in high season reservations may be hard to come by, especially at Walt Disney World and in popular beach resorts. Book well in advance: even a year may not be too much for the Christmas and Easter holidays.

American hotels and motels usually charge by the room, not the number of occupants, but hard-sell advertising may quote a per person rate. State and sometimes local taxes are added to the bill (see p. 66). Most rooms have two double beds, private bathroom (a shower in budget motels) and colour TV. There may be a refrigerator and cooking facilities.

'Efficiencies' are small apartments with kitchenette or separate kitchen and dining area. Facilities include dishes, pans and cutlery. In recent years, tour operators have been offering more and more self-catering villas and apartments.

In coastal areas, the further from the beach you go, the lower the rates should be. Rooms facing a pool or garden are often two-thirds the price of rooms with an ocean view.

High season in Florida is from 15 December to March or April (including Easter). Quietest times are in May and June and between September and November, when prices are generally lower. Some resort hotels offer special rates to guests who take meals on the premises: American Plan includes three meals a day and the Modified American Plan, either breakfast, lunch or dinner.

Larger hotels employ a concierge/bell captain who can arrange tours, call a cab or hire a car for you, but you may be able to economize by making your own arrangements.

AIRPORTS

Miami International Airport (MIA) is a crowded and confusing place, just west of the city centre. Served by more than 60 airlines, it's one of the world's busiest airports, with two terminals connected by an automated 'peoplemover'. The main terminal, divided into concourses (or zones), has two floors, the lower level for arrivals and baggage claim and the upper for departures and ticketing. Here you'll find bars, fast-food restaurants, telephones, shops and an information desk open 24 hours a day. If you're not well supplied with dollars, change money at one of the exchange counters. It's unwise to go into town without sufficient US currency.

Orlando (McCoy) International Airport (ORL or MCO) is spacious, glittering and constantly expanding. There are two terminals, each with shops, restaurants and exchange counters. Automatic trains shuttle people to satellite gates. No trolleys are provided so suitcases with wheels are recommended.

At both airports, red and green customs channels are in operation and formalities are generally simple and quick.

Ground transport. From Miami International, a taxi to Miami Beach usually takes 15–25 minutes (up to an hour during rush hour). The bright blue vehicles of the Airport Region Taxi Service (ARTS) carry passengers to nearby destinations for a low, flat fare. 'Red Top' minibuses will take you to almost any hotel downtown or on Miami Beach for a third of the taxi fare. Cheaper still are the municipal buses, leaving every 30–45 minutes from the main terminal's lower level. The Tri-Rail system runs to Gold Coast resorts.

From Orlando International, taxis and shuttle minibuses operate to downtown Orlando, International Drive and Walt Disney World and to Cocoa Beach. Some hotels run a free shuttle. A municipal bus runs to downtown Orlando.

Check-in time. Arrive at least 45 minutes before domestic flights, and one hour before international flights. (The airlines suggest two hours.) For flight information, call your airline. **117**

Other Florida airports. Fort Lauderdale, West Palm Beach, Key West and Tampa have their own international airports and several other cities are served by domestic flights.

Domestic Flights. Air travel is by far the quickest and most convenient way of getting round the US. A few of the most-travelled routes have shuttle services. Travellers from abroad can buy a Visit USA ticket, which provides substantial discounts and sets no fixed programme. These must be bought before you arrive in the US (or within 15 days of arrival).

Fares change constantly, so it is wise to consult a travel agent for the latest information about special deals.

B

BICYCLE HIRE

Popular beach resorts have shops which hire out bicycles by the hour, day or week. They are an ideal way to get around Key West, for example, with its parking problems and short distances. There are few segregated cycle tracks (Coconut Grove is an exception). Make sure a lock is included and check on insurance against theft.

C

CAMPING

Camping in America generally involves recreational vehicles ('RVs') – campers, motor homes or caravans (trailers). If you are camping the American way, the *Rand McNally Campground and Trailer Park Guide* or the voluminous *Woodalls* list and grade campgrounds according to their facilities. (A campsite in the US means the actual spot where you put your RV or tent.) The *Florida State Parks Guide,* a map of all the excellent state parks and state

118 recreational areas with camping facilities, is available from:

The Florida Department of Natural Resources
Bureau of Education and Information
3900 Commonwealth Boulevard
Tallahassee, FL 32399-3000

In each state park, your length of stay is limited to two weeks. To avoid disappointment, reserve a place in advance by telephone.

Camping beside the road – or on private land without permission – is both illegal and unsafe.

CAR HIRE

Hot competition among car hire companies ('car rental companies' in the US) keeps rates relatively low, and automatic and air-conditioned cars are the norm. If you can pick up and return the car at the same place, try one of the local businesses. If you plan to drop it off in another city, it's best to reserve a car before you get to the US at one of the international companies – it will be cheaper.

The well-known car hire agencies charge higher rental rates, but may include insurance costs in the price: small companies, with little or no insurance included in the rates, offer what may sound fairly expensive insurance coverage. One way or another, you are recommended to make sure you have 'CDW' (collision damage waiver), or you will have to pay for some or all of the cost of repairs.

Many inclusive holidays and fly-drive packages promise a 'free car', but you will usually have to pay Florida taxes and CDW when you collect it.

Drivers over 21 with a valid driving licence can hire a car. Some agencies make exceptions for 18-year-old drivers paying with a credit card. For tourists from non-English-speaking countries, a translation of the driving licence may be requested, together with the national licence itself, or failing this, an International Driving Permit.

Invariably, it is more convenient to pay with a major credit card rather than cash. If you have no card, you must leave a large deposit. Sometimes cash is refused at night and on weekends. To extend your hire, inform the original office, or stop at the nearest branch office. **119**

CHILDREN'S FLORIDA

There should be no problem keeping children happy, whether at the many and varied theme parks or on the beaches (the Gulf Coast generally has calmer water and safe, gently sloping sands). Most hotels and many motels have pools. The sun, heat and humidity can take their toll, especially in the form of dehydration, so make sure your children get plenty to drink. American restaurants are used to accommodating all ages, but when you want to escape, large hotels can provide babysitters.

CLIMATE

Most of the year Florida weather ranges from warm to hot, but the coasts are agreeably cooled by sea breezes. The peak tourist season is winter, when temperatures and rainfall are at their lowest. You may encounter a brief spell of cool weather, but not often cold enough to interfere with swimming and sunbathing. From June to October it's hot and humid, and you can expect some rain most days, though rarely so persistent as to be troublesome.

Some tourist brochures boast that you'll never need warm clothing, even in the middle of winter, but prudence suggests otherwise. In winter, Atlantic beaches can be very windy, and there may be some rainy days and cold spells. Even in the south temperatures *can* dip to near freezing for short periods, though many winter days see temperatures in the 80s, especially in south Florida and on the Keys.

Hurricanes hardly ever happen. On average, Florida is hit only one year in seven and only between June and November, so your chance of being in the wrong place at the wrong time is minimal.

For a weather report, dial 661-5065 in Miami.

Average daytime temperatures for Miami (the US still sticks to the Fahrenheit scale):

	J	F	M	A	M	J	J	A	S	O	N	D
°C	21	21	22	24	26	27	28	29	27	26	23	2
°F	69	70	71	74	78	81	82	84	81	78	73	70

CLOTHING

Whenever it's hot or humid, Floridians turn on the air conditioners. These can blow with arctic chill, so don't forget to take a wrap with you when shopping, dining out or riding in air-conditioned vehicles – including city buses. Winter can bring surprisingly cold spells, so be ready for any eventuality.

In resorts, casual wear is appropriate round the clock, something light, bright, loose and made of cotton rather than artificial fibres. Palm Beach is an exception, favouring crisp, conservative and – for men – nautical fashions. If you're likely to go swimming often, pack spare swimwear for a rapid change. Other useful items to bring include an umbrella, sunhat and comfortable sports-type shoes for tramping round theme parks or along rocky trails.

COMPLAINTS

If you have a serious complaint about business practices and have talked with the manager of the establishment in question to no avail, you may contact the Agriculture Department:

Consumer Services Division
The Capitol, Tallahassee
Florida, FL 32301
Tel. 1-800-342-2176

CRIME

See also EMERGENCIES. Buying and selling illegal drugs is a serious offence. Florida has a large force of undercover officers (plain-clothes police) who are battling to keep drugs out.

Most hotels have a safe for valuables. Never leave money, credit cards, cheque books, cameras, etc., in a hotel room, but always in the safe.

In Miami, beware of pickpockets on city buses, in queues, crowded stores and elevators (lifts). The Miami police warn you to drive with windows up and doors locked, especially in areas with numerous traffic lights. Would-be thieves may stage fake accidents or tell you there's something wrong with your car to get you to stop.

An unfortunate trend in the Miami area – and part of a world-wide big-city phenomenon – is the increase in crimes of violence. **121**

To be on the safe side, go out after dark in groups, not alone, and avoid carrying large amounts of cash or valuables. It's a good idea to leave your car with the attendant at a restaurant, nightclub or discotheque, rather than parking it yourself on a dimly lit side street. If you use normal common sense and avoid certain areas, especially Liberty City in north-west Miami, then you need not feel apprehensive.

CUSTOMS AND ENTRY REGULATIONS

UK citizens and some other foreign visitors no longer require a visa to enter the US, and instead can obtain a visa waiver form from their travel agent or airline. Canadians need only provide evidence of their nationality. Citizens of the Republic of Ireland, Australia, New Zealand and South Africa need a visa (but rules change, so check with your local US embassy or consulate, or travel agent). The application process can be slow, depending on individual circumstances. When you apply, you may have to produce documents which show that you intend to return home.

Duty-free allowance. You will be asked to complete a customs declaration form before you arrive in the US. The chart shows what main duty-free items you may take into the US (if you are over 21) and, when returning home, into your own country.

Into:	Cigarettes		Cigars		Tobacco	Spirits		Wine
US	200	or	50	or	1,350 g	1 l.	or	1 l.
Australia	200	or	250 g	or	250 g	1 l.	or	1 l.
Canada	200	and	50	and	900 g	1.1 l.	or	1.1 l.
Eire	200	or	50	or	250 g	1 l.	and	2 l.
N. Zealand	200	or	50	or	250 g	1.1 l.	and	4.5 l.
S. Africa	400	and	50	and	250 g	1 l.	and	2 l.
UK	200	or	50	or	250 g	1 l.	and	2 l.

A non-resident may claim, free of duty and taxes, articles up to $100 in value for use as gifts. Plants and foodstuffs are subject to strict control; visitors from abroad may not import fruits, vegetables, meat or liqueur chocolates.

Arriving and departing passengers should report any money or cheques exceeding a total of $10,000.

D

DISABLED TRAVELLERS

More efforts have been made in the United States than almost any other country to enable those with disabilities to get around. Hotels and public buildings have wheelchair entrances and special toilets. Theme parks make as many of their attractions as possible accessible to wheelchairs and some provide special help to sight- and hearing-impaired visitors.

DRIVING

Drive on the right. In Florida, you may turn right after stopping at a red light, provided there is no cross-traffic, you have given way to pedestrians and there is no sign to the contrary. Never drive at night without headlights: it's strictly illegal. Switch on headlights also when it rains enough for wipers to be needed. Front seat belts must be worn and you must carry your driving licence.

Lane discipline differs from European norms. American drivers tend to stick to one lane, making no distinction between 'fast' or 'slow' lanes except to some extent on the Interstate network. You may therefore be overtaken on either side, so don't change lanes without careful checking. In populated areas, the middle lane is generally for making left turns only.

Don't drink and drive – driving while intoxicated ('DWI') may get you locked up.

Expressways (motorways). On the high-speed divided highways called expressways, driving follows certain rules. Rather than accelerate up the ramp (slip road) to join the traffic at its own speed, you hesitate at the top of the ramp and wait for an opening. A national speed limit of 55 mph (88 kph) operates on highways, except on expressways in rural areas, where the limit is 65 mph (105 kph). Other limits such as 45 mph (72 kph) apply where indicated. If you keep up with the flow of traffic, you'll have no problem, but go any faster, and a patrol car may pull you over. You can, at least, take comfort in the knowledge that American police are generally kind to foreigners.

If you have a breakdown on an expressway, pull over on to the right-hand shoulder, tie a handkerchief to the door handle or radio aerial, raise the bonnet (hood) and wait in the car for assistance. At night, use the hazard warning lights.

Tolls. In Florida tolls are collected at turnpikes, and at many bridges and causeways. Keep a supply of coins when travelling; most toll areas provide a basket into which you drop the right change, so there's no waiting.

Petrol (gas) and services. Florida's service stations have both self-service and full-service pumps, fuel at the latter being much more expensive. They offer regular, middle and premium grades – standard is adequate for most rental cars. In some areas it is necessary to pre-pay, especially at night. Some pumps are operated by inserting a credit card (and major international cards are accepted). Note that many stations close in the evenings and on Sundays.

Most rental cars in Florida are equipped with air conditioners; if your car is running low on fuel or overheating, turn off the 'air con' – it's a strain on the engine.

Parking. Florida's famous attractions usually have large and inexpensive (rarely free) car parks. Most municipal car parks have meters; the coins required and the times of operation are always noted on them. Spaces in the streets are indicated by white lines painted on the road. Your car must point in the direction of the flow of traffic, or nose-in where angle-parking is indicated. (Florida cars don't have number plates in front.) Do not park by a fire hydrant or a **124** kerb painted yellow or red.

Directions. Try to get help planning your route if you don't know the area you are heading for. Don't assume that if you hit the right number street, avenue or road you can continue to your destination. It may come to a dead end or pass through undesirable places. The expressways are usually the quickest way of crossing the big cities.

Note that road numbers are generally even for east-west routes, odd for north-south.

The American Automobile Association offers assistance to members of affiliated organizations abroad. It also provides travel information for the US and can arrange automobile insurance by the month for owner-drivers. Contact the AAA at 1000 AAA Drive, Heathrow, FL 32746-5063; tel. (407) 444-7000.

Road signs. Although the US has begun to change over to international road signs, progress is gradual. Some of the terms used may be unfamiliar or confusing.

Detour	Diversion
Divided highway	Dual carriageway
No passing	No overtaking
Railroad crossing	Level crossing
Traffic circle	Roundabout
Yield	Give way

E

ELECTRIC CURRENT
The US uses 110–115 volt 60-cycle A.C. Plugs are small, flat and two- or three-pronged; foreigners will need an adaptor for shavers, etc.

EMBASSIES AND CONSULATES
Few English-speaking countries maintain a consulate in Florida.

Australia:	636 5th Avenue, New York
	Tel. (212) 245-4000
Canada:	1251 Avenue of the Americas, New York
	Tel. (212) 586-2400

Eire:	515 Madison Avenue New York
	Tel. (212) 319-2555
New Zealand:	Suite 530, 630 5th Avenue, New York
	Tel. (212) 586-0060
South Africa:	425 Park Avenue, New York
	Tel. (212) 838-1700
United Kingdom:	225 Peachtree St NE, Atlanta, Georgia
	Tel. (404) 524-5856

(The office in Miami is for trade matters only: Suite 2110 Brickell Bay Tower, 1001 S. Bayshore Drive, Miami; tel. (305) 374 1522.)

EMERGENCIES

See also MEDICAL CARE and POLICE. Dial 911, and the operator will ask if you want police, ambulance or the fire department.

All towns and cities have a 24-hour number to call in case of emergency, if you need either a doctor or a dentist. For a doctor in the Miami area, phone 324-8717. For a dentist the number is 667-3647.

ETIQUETTE

Many Americans are very polite, saying 'Sir' and 'Ma'am' to strangers and service staff. Oddly enough, though, requests often consist of 'Gimme' and 'I need', unaccompanied by 'please'. 'Thank you' always receives a response such as 'You're welcome' (or 'You're quite welcome', 'quite' meaning 'very').

GETTING TO FLORIDA

Because fares and conditions change frequently, it is advisable to consult travel agents for the latest information on fares and other arrangements.

From North America

BY AIR: Miami, Fort Lauderdale, West Palm Beach, Orlando (the airport closest to Walt Disney World), Tampa, St Petersburg and

Sarasota are easily accessible from the larger US cities, with many non-stop flights daily to major centres.

BY BUS: Florida destinations are linked to all major centres by Greyhound, which has merged with its previous main rival, Trailways.

BY RAIL: Amtrak advertises a variety of bargain fares, including Excursion and Family fares and tour packages with hotel and guide included. It runs a car-carrying train between Lorton near Washington DC and Sanford near Orlando.

BY CAR: Travellers coming down the east coast can take I-95 via Washington and Savannah. The shortest route from the west is I-10, passing Tucson, El Paso, Houston and Mobile.

From the UK

BY AIR: There are several daily non-stop flights from Heathrow and Gatwick to Miami, as well as other non-stops to Orlando.

From other European cities

Non-stop flights operate from Frankfurt to Orlando and Miami, from Amsterdam to Orlando, and from Paris, Madrid, Rome and Milan to Miami. There are many one-stop flights from other points.

Fares available include first class, economy, Excursion, APEX (Advance Purchase Excursion), Super-APEX and special 'ticket sales' available through travel agents. In general, the longer ahead you book, the lower the fare, with the exception of stand-by fares which apply only at certain times of year.

Some US airlines offer travellers from abroad a discount on the cost of internal flights, or flat-rate, unlimited-travel tickets for specific periods.

Charter Flights and Package Tours. Most charter flights must be booked and paid for well in advance. Many package tours are available: camper holidays, coach tours, excursions to Walt Disney World or the Bahamas, trips to other American cities and sights, etc. Most Caribbean cruises originate in Florida ports.

Some two-centre holidays divide their time between Orlando and one of the beaches (east or west coast). Other combinations offer Orlando plus a short cruise or a spell on a Caribbean island.

Baggage. You may check in, free, two suitcases of normal size. One piece of hand luggage which fits under the aircraft seat may also be carried on board. Confirm size and weight restrictions with your travel agent or airline when booking your ticket.

It is advisable to insure all luggage for the duration of your trip, preferably as part of a general travel insurance policy. Any travel agent can arrange this.

GUIDES AND TOURS

Some of the larger attractions provide the services of a guide. At Walt Disney World's Magic Kingdom, for example, ask at the Town Hall. Foreign-language guides are on call to take visitors on a quick tour, including a selection of rides.

Sightseeing tours by bus or 'tram' are available in most cities and resorts. One-day bus tours from Miami to Disney World are not recommended – they don't allow enough time once you get there.

Pleasure cruises operate from many resorts, touring the coast, the inlets, lakes, rivers and swamps, some serving meals on board or stopping at a restaurant. Miami and Miami Beach are well served, with tours and cruises of varying lengths up and down the coast. At Key Largo, you can take a glass-bottomed boat to view the coral reefs. Tours and cruises are also available in Fort Lauderdale, West Palm Beach, St Petersburg, Sarasota, Naples, Tarpon Springs and Key West.

LANGUAGE

Miami is virtually a bilingual city, and such has been the influence of refugees, mainly from Cuba, that you'll hear as much Spanish as English.

Most English-speaking foreigners are familiar with American words and phrases. However, here are a few which can cause confusion.

US	British	US	British
admission	**entry fee**	minister	**vicar**
bathroom	**toilet**	no admission	**free entry**
bill	**note (money)**	purse	**handbag**
billfold	**wallet**	rest room	**toilet**
check	**bill (restaurant)**	round-trip ticket	**return ticket**
collect call	**reverse charges**	second floor	**first floor**
elevator	**lift**	sidewalk	**pavement**
first floor	**ground floor**	stand in line	**queue up**
gas	**petrol**	trailer	**caravan**
liquor	**spirits**	underpass	**subway**
liquor store	**off-licence**		

LAUNDRY AND DRY-CLEANING

Most larger hotels offer these services, at a price. Some hotels have coin-operated washing machines and dryers.

LOST PROPERTY

Air, rail and bus terminals and many stores have special 'lost and found' areas. Restaurants put aside lost articles in the hope that someone will claim them. If your lost property is valuable contact the police. If you lose your passport, get in touch with your consulate immediately.

MAPS

Welcome stations on main highways and ports of entry hand out free maps, and the local chamber of commerce or tourist authority will give or sell you maps with attractions marked on them. Service stations dispense maps from vending machines, and quite good maps are given out when you hire a car. The maps in this book were prepared by Falk-Verlag.

MEDICAL CARE

See also EMERGENCIES. Foreigners should note the US doesn't provide free medical services, and that treatment is expensive. Arrangements should therefore be made in advance for temporary health insurance (through a travel agent or an insurance company).

'Health-First' clinics offer less prohibitively expensive treatment than private practitioners. Emergency rooms of hospitals will treat anyone in need of speedy attention, including hospitalization in a community ward. If you arrive in Florida after flying through several time zones, take it easy the first couple of days. Doctors recommend that visitors eat lightly initially, and get plenty of rest.

Beware of the powerful sun. Start with a high protection factor (20 or more) sunscreen or sunblock, and build up a tan gradually in small doses. Drink plenty of water. It is all too easy to become dehydrated – the warning signs are headaches, lassitude (and grumpy children).

Visitors from the UK will find that some medicines sold over the counter at home can only be bought on prescription in the US. There's no shortage of drugstores, or pharmacies; a few of them stay open late at night.

MONEY MATTERS

Currency. The dollar is divided into 100 cents.

Banknotes: $1, $2 (rare), $5, $10, $20, $50 and $100. Larger denominations are not in general circulation. All notes are the same size and colour, so beware of mixing them up.

Coins: 1¢ (called a 'penny'), 5¢ ('nickel'), 10¢ ('dime'), 25¢ ('quarter'), 50¢ ('half dollar') and $1. Only the first four are commonly used. You may inadvertently be given Canadian or other foreign coins in your change. Canadian coins are worth about 15% less than US ones, and they do not work in automatic machines such as telephones.

Banks and currency exchange. Banking hours are usually from 9 a.m. to 2 or 3 p.m., Monday to Friday, but take note that very few banks change foreign currency. Walt Disney World's banks are a notable exception. Even in major cities, there may be only one counter in one bank able to handle foreign money. American hotel receptionists are distrustful of foreign banknotes, and they may offer a low exchange rate (so be aware of the exact rate before changing money). It is simpler to carry US dollar traveller's cheques, major credit cards and some cash in dollars.

When changing money or traveller's cheques, ask for $20 notes, which are accepted everywhere, as some establishments will refuse larger notes unless they nearly equal the amount to be paid. In fact $100 notes seem to circulate more outside the US than inside, fakes included.

Credit cards. When shopping or paying hotel bills, you may be asked: 'Cash or charge?', meaning you have the choice of paying in cash or by credit card. Businesses are wary of little-known cards, but most accept the top American or international cards. You'll often need some form of identification when charging your purchase.

Many service stations and other businesses will not take money at night, only cards. Outside normal office hours, it's sometimes impossible to rent cars and pay bills with cash.

Traveller's cheques. These are safer than cash. They can quickly be exchanged, as long as they are in US dollars. Banks will usually want to see your passport or other form of identity document ('ID'), but many hotels, shops and restaurants will accept them directly in lieu of cash, especially those issued by American banks. Change only small amounts at a time: keep the balance of your cheques in your hotel safe if possible and make a note of serial numbers, and where and when you used each cheque.

Prices. Most displayed prices do not include a state sales tax of around 6% – it's added when you pay. The same applies to your hotel bill, which may be further increased by local taxes.

Prices vary considerably in the US. For moderately priced goods, visit the big department or discount stores. Small independent grocery stores, drugstores and 24-hour 'convenience stores' have price mark-ups of 10–70% over the supermarkets, but independent service stations are cheaper than those of the large oil companies.

NEWSPAPERS AND MAGAZINES

Local newspapers and the national daily *US Today* are sold in drug-stores and from vending machines. Special newsstands carry the *New York Times* and the *Wall Street Journal,* as well as a variety of other newspapers. Two daily papers are printed in Miami: the *Miami Herald* (*El Nuovo Miami Herald* in Spanish) and the *Diario Las Américas.* The *Orlando Sentinel* provides information about Central Florida. A local paper will put you in touch with community news and list TV programmes, opening hours of attractions, grocery-store bargains, etc. Some papers also give coupons for price reductions at various restaurants. Except for the local Spanish-language papers, you are unlikely to come across publications in other languages unless you seek them out.

Most Florida cities have their own magazines with articles on events. Look for free 'What's On' type magazines in hotels (for example *Welcome to Miami and the Beaches*).

OPENING HOURS

Most shops and businesses are open from 8 or 9 a.m. (larger stores from 9.30 or 10 a.m.) to 5 or 6 p.m. Some stores and chain-restaurants never close. Small restaurants usually open at 6 a.m. and close by 11 p.m.

Below are listed the opening hours of some of the sites mentioned in this guide. However, it's worth telephoning ahead of time to check. In many cases, hours are extended during holiday periods.

Miami

Ancient Spanish Monastery. Monday–Saturday 10 a.m.–5 p.m.,
Sunday 12 noon–5 p.m.
Bass Museum of Art. Tuesday–Saturday 10 a.m.–5 p.m.,
Sunday 12 noon–5 p.m.

Fairchild Tropical Garden. Daily 9.30 a.m.–4.30 p.m.
Lowe Art Museum. Tuesday–Saturday 10 a.m.–5 p.m.,
Sunday 12 noon–5 p.m.
Metro-Dade Cultural Center. Monday–Saturday 10 a.m.–5 p.m.,
(except Thursdays 10 a.m.–9 p.m.), Sunday 12 noon–5 p.m.
Metrozoo. Temporarily closed. See p. 35 for further details.
Monkey Jungle. Daily 9.30 a.m.–5 p.m.
Museum of Science and Planetarium. Daily 10 a.m.–6 p.m.
Orchid Jungle. Daily 8.30 a.m.–5.30 p.m.
Parrot Jungle. Daily 9.30 a.m.–6 p.m.
Seaquarium. Daily 9.30 a.m.–6.00 p.m. Box office closes at 4.30 p.m.
Vizcaya. Daily 9.30 a.m.–5 p.m. Closed Christmas Day.

Fort Lauderdale
Ocean World. Daily from 10 a.m. Box office closes at 4.15 p.m.

Fort Myers
Edison Winter Home. Monday–Saturday 9 a.m.–4 p.m.,
Sunday 12.30 a.m.–4 p.m. Closed Thanksgiving (fourth Thursday in
November) and Christmas.

Kennedy Space Center
Daily 9 a.m.–7 p.m. Last bus tour 4.30 p.m. Closed Christmas Day.

Key West
Ernest Hemingway House. Daily 9 a.m.–5 p.m.
Key West Lighthouse. Daily 9.30 a.m.–5 p.m.
Truman Little White House. Daily 9 a.m.–5 p.m.

Orlando
Sea World. Daily 9.a.m.–7 p.m. Extended hours seasonally.
Universal Studios. 9 a.m.–11 p.m. Opening times vary seasonally.
Walt Disney World. Ride and attractions open daily from 9 a.m.
but it's worth arriving by 8.30 a.m.
Closing times vary from park to park and season to season,
from 6 p.m. to 11 p.m.
Wet 'n' Wild. Daily 10 a.m. 5 p.m. in spring and autumn,
9 a.m.–10 or 11 p.m. in summer.

Palm Beach/West Palm Beach
Flagler Museum. Tuesday–Saturday 10 a.m.–5 p.m.,
Sunday 12 noon–5 p.m.
Lion Country Safari. Daily 9.30 a.m.–5 p.m. Gate closes at 4.30 p.m.
Norton Gallery of Art. Tuesday–Saturday 10 a.m.–5 p.m., Sunday 1–5 p.m.

St Augustine
Castillo de San Marcos. Daily 8.30 a.m.–5.30 p.m.
Closed Christmas Day.

St Petersburg
Museum of Fine Arts. Tuesday–Saturday 10 a.m.–5 p.m.,
Sunday 1–5 p.m.
Salvador Dali Museum. Tuesday–Saturday 10 a.m.–5 p.m.,
Sunday 12 noon–5 p.m.

Sarasota
Bellm's Cars and Music of Yesterday.
Monday–Saturday 8.30 a.m.–6 p.m., Sunday 9.30 a.m.–6 p.m.
Ringling Museums. Daily 10 a.m.–5.30 p.m.
Thursdays to 10 p.m. from October to June.

Tampa
Busch Gardens. Daily 9.30 a.m.–6 p.m.
Extended hours during holidays, summer.

Winter Haven
Cypress Gardens. Daily 9 a.m.–6 p.m. Extended hours certain periods.

P

PHOTOGRAPHY AND VIDEO
Camera shops sell film, but drugstores and supermarkets supply
the same at discount prices. Wait until you are home to develop
transparency film because it may take longer than you think. Do not
store film in the car: it may get so hot that film will be damaged.

Airport security X-ray machines are safe for normal film, whether exposed or unused. Super-fast film may be affected and you should ask for separate inspection.

Video tape is available for all types of camera. Note that pre-recorded tapes bought in the US will not function on European systems (and vice versa). The same applies to the video cameras you can rent at some attractions. Tapes can be converted, but only at considerable expense.

PLANNING YOUR BUDGET

To give you an idea of what to expect, here's a list of average prices. However, they must be taken as broad guidelines, as inflation gradually pushes prices upwards.

Airport Transfer. Taxi from Miami International Airport to downdown Miami $15; to Miami Beach up to $25. Red Top Sedan Service $8–13, depending on destination.

Taxi from Orlando International Airport to International Drive $22, shuttle $11; to Walt Disney World $38, shuttle $14.

Baby-sitters. $4–5 per hour for one or two children; $1 for each additional child, plus transport expenses. Hotels charge $6–8 per hour.

Bicycle hire. $3 per hour; $5–15 per day; $20–35 per week.

Campground. $10–25 per day, per site (i.e. space).

Car hire. Prices vary widely with the company and the season, and depend on what insurance is included (see p. 119). A typical price for a mid-size car with unlimited mileage, fully insured, high season might be $36 per day, $169 per week.

Cigarettes. Pack of 20: American $2, foreign brands higher.

Diving. Half-day from boat $40; diving school $100/day.

Entertainment. Cinema $4–8; nightclub/discotheque $5–20 cover charge, $4–6 drinks; dinner show $30–50.

Golf. $25–80 (including cart).

Hairdressers. Man's haircut $7–25; Woman's haircut $10–25; cut, shampoo and set $15–30; colouring $10–50.

Hotels. Double room with bath: de luxe $120 and up; medium price $70–100; budget $40–60. Motels $25–50. There are big seasonal variations.

Laundry. Shirt $1.90; blouse $3.75.

Dry-cleaning. Jacket $4.50 and up; trousers $2.50 and up; dress $6 and up.

Meals and drinks. Continental breakfast $2–3; full breakfast $4–9; lunch in snack bar $4–6; in restaurant $8–14; dinner $15–30 (more with entertainment); fast-food meal $3–5; coffee $1; beer $2.50–3.50; glass of wine $3–5; carafe $6–10; bottle $10–20; cocktail $4–6.

Museums. $4–10.

Petrol (gasoline). $1.05 per US gallon (approx. 4 litres).

Swamp airboat rides. $5–8 (45 minutes); glass-bottom boat $14.

Taxis. Meters start at $1.25, then $1.40 per mile (more in Orlando).

Theme Parks. Busch gardens $22.50; Kennedy Space Center free, bus tours $7; IMAX film $4; Parrot Jungle $11; Sea World $30; Wet 'n' Wild $20; Universal Studios $32.

Walt Disney World: one-day ticket (Magic Kingdom *or* Disney-MGM Studios *or* EPCOT Center) adult $36, child 3–9 $28; four-day Super Pass (all parks) adult $125, child $100; five-day Super Duper Pass (all parks and other facilities) adult $170, child $135.

In general, children's tickets are anything from 50% to 100% of adult rate.

POLICE

City police are concerned with local crime and traffic violations, while Highway Patrol officers (also called State Troopers) ensure highway safety, and are on the lookout for people speeding or driving under the influence of alcohol or drugs. American police officers are usually very fair and friendly. For emergencies, dial 911 (fire, police, ambulance).

POST OFFICES

The US postal service deals only with mail; telephone and telegraph services are operated by other companies. Post letters in the blue kerbside boxes. You can buy stamps from machines in post office entrance halls after hours. Stamps from machines in hotels and shops cost a lot more than face value.

Post office hours are from 8 a.m. to 5 p.m., Monday to Friday, from 8 a.m. to 12 noon on Saturdays. In larger towns, one branch usually remains open later in the evening, till 9 p.m. or so.

Poste restante (general delivery). You can have mail marked 'General Delivery' sent to you care of the main post office of any town. The letters will be held for no more than a month. Take your driving licence or passport with you for identification.

PUBLIC HOLIDAYS

If a holiday, such as Christmas Day, falls on a Sunday, banks and most stores close on the following day. At long weekends (such as the one following Thanksgiving), offices are closed for four days. Many restaurants never shut, however, even at Christmas.

New Years Day	**1 January**
Martin Luther King Day	**Third Monday in January**
Washington's Birthday*	**Third Monday in February**
Memorial Day	**Last Monday in May**
Independence Day	**4 July**
Labor Day	**First Monday in September**
Columbus Day*	**Second Monday in October**
Veterans' Day	**11 November**
Thanksgiving Day	**Fourth Thursday in November**
Christmas Day	**25 December**

*Shops and businesses open

R

RADIO AND TV

Numerous AM and FM radio stations broadcast pop, rock and Country and Western music; most large cities also have a classical station.

Almost every hotel room has a television carrying many channels, some 24 hours a day. Local news begins around 6 p.m., with national and international news from New York at 6.30 or 7 p.m. CNN transmits news around the clock.

Commercial American television aims to appeal to the largest possible audience, and the amount of advertising tends to annoy those who are not familiar with it. The exceptions are PBS channels (Public Broadcasting Service), which screen music, drama, information and educational programmes including imports from the UK and the MacNeil-Lehrer News Hour from 7–8 p.m. A variety of special-interest shows and films are aired on cable channels (some piped free to hotel rooms).

RELIGION

Saturday newspapers often list the church services of the following day, with details of visiting preachers. Besides Catholic, Episcopalian, Presbyterian and Methodist churches there are many fundamentalist and southern Baptist denominations. In Miami Beach and along the Gold Coast there are numerous synagogues and there's at least one in every main town.

S

SMOKING

Smoking is banned in many public buildings and places of entertainment, including the attractions, rides and waiting areas in theme parks. Most restaurants have smoking and non-smoking areas: you will be asked which you want. Many hotels have non-smoking rooms.

TAXIS. See TRANSPORT.

TELEPHONES

American telephone companies are efficient and reliable. Dialling directions are always posted beside public telephones.

Local calls. Lift the receiver, deposit 25¢ in the slot, wait for the dialling tone, then dial the seven-digit number. The operator will automatically inform you of any additional charge, so have some change ready. For local directory inquiries, dial 411. For local operator assistance, and for help within the same area code, dial 0.

Long-distance calls may be dialled direct from a pay phone if you follow the posted directions. The prefix 1- usually has to be dialled before the number. If you don't know the correct area code, dial 00 for operator assistance. Long-distance calls cost more from a pay phone than from a private one. International direct dial calls require the prefix 011, then the country code.

Telephone rates are listed in the introduction to the white pages of the telephone directory, along with information on personal (person-to-person), reverse-charge (collect) and credit card calls. Some telephone companies no longer accept the major credit cards. All numbers with an 800 prefix are toll-free.

Fax. You can send faxes from many hotels, and from office service bureaux found in some shopping malls.

Telegrams. American telegraph companies offer domestic and overseas services, as well as telex facilities, and are listed in the yellow pages. You can telephone the telegraph office, dictate the message and have the charge added to your hotel bill, or dictate it from a coin-operated phone and pay on the spot. A letter telegram (night letter) costs about half the rate of a normal telegram. Note that the UK does not have a telegram service: your message will just be delivered with the mail. **139**

TIME DIFFERENCES

The continental US has four time zones; Florida (like New York City) is on Eastern Standard Time. Between April and October, Daylight Saving Time is adopted and clocks move ahead one hour. The following chart shows the time in various cities in winter when it's noon in Florida:

Los Angeles	**Miami**	London	Sydney
9 a.m. Sunday	**noon Sunday**	5 p.m. Sunday	4 a.m. Monday

TIPPING

Waiters and waitresses earn most of their salary from tips; often they are paid little else. In simple eating houses you usually pay the cashier on your way out, after leaving a tip on the table. Otherwise, you can write in the tip on a credit card slip: they always leave a space for it. Cinema or theatre ushers and filling-station attendants are not tipped.

Some suggestions:

Guide	10–15%
Hairdresser/barber	15%
Hotel porter (per bag)	50¢–$1 (minimum $1)
Taxi driver	15%
Waiter	15–20% (unless service has been added – a growing trend)

TOILETS

You can find toilets in restaurants, railway stations and large stores, as well as hotels and restaurants. In some places you must deposit a dime, in others you can leave a tip for the attendant if there is one.

Americans use the terms 'rest room', 'powder room', 'bathroom' (private) and 'ladies' or 'men's room' to indicate the toilet.

TOURIST INFORMATION AGENCIES

For information before your trip, write to:

United States Travel & Tourism Administration
22 Sackville Street, London W1X 2EA
Tel. 071-439 7433

Florida Division of Tourism in Europe
1st floor, 18–24 Westbourne Grove
London W2 5RH
Tel. 071-727 1661

State of Florida Division of Tourism, Visitor Inquiries
126 W. Van Buren Street, Tallahassee, FL 32399-2000
Tel. (904) 487-1462

Information is also freely dispensed from welcome stations at the main entry points to the state, in hotels and elsewhere, but the chief source of tourist information in any town is the local chamber of commerce.

TRANSPORT. See also AIRPORTS, GETTING TO FLORIDA, CAR HIRE and DRIVING.

Buses. See also GUIDES AND TOURS. The largest company, Greyhound Lines, has merged with its rival Trailways, and serves all major resorts and attractions. As well as the state-wide network, it offers services to and from cities all over the US. (New York to Orlando takes around 25 hours.) Smaller bus lines provide local shuttle services between hotels and attractions, as well as sightseeing tours. Visitors can buy unlimited rover passes (these can only be bought outside the US), valid for a specified length of time, to go anywhere in the country by Greyhound bus at a flat rate.

City buses. Rule number one: have the exact change ready to deposit in the box beside the driver. Miami buses can be crowded and frantic, but generally speaking, service is regular and punctual.

Miami Metrorail. Miami has an elevated railway running north-south through the centre of the city. The air-conditioned trains operate at frequent intervals from 5.30 a.m. to midnight.

Taxis. Taxis always carry a roof sign and can easily be recognized. Most have meters, and the rates are generally marked on the doors. Some cruise the streets, especially in city centres. To phone for a taxi, look in the yellow pages under 'Taxicabs'. Tip 15% of the fare.

Trains. Amtrak (National Railroad Passenger Corporation) offers a variety of bargain fares, including Excursion and Family fares; the USA Railpass can only be purchased abroad, but many package tours are available in the US. Air-conditioned trains link Florida's main towns with urban centres throughout the US. (New York to Orlando takes 24 hours.) The Tri-Rail system connects Miami and the international airport with Gold Coast cities and resorts.

VACCINATIONS

No vaccinations are required or recommended by health authorities.

WEIGHTS AND MEASURES

The United States is one of the last countries in the world to adopt the metric system, and is not yet involved in an official changeover programme.

YOUTH HOSTELS

There are only about 160 hostels in the US. Most are outside the big cities, and the distances between them can be enormous. Some budget hotels offer a large discount to International YHA (Youth Hostel Association) members. There is no age limit. For further information, apply to:

American Youth Hostel Association, Inc.

National Campus, Delaplane, VA 22025

Index